So You Want to Write a Children's Book

A Step-By-Step Guide to Writing and Publishing for Kids

REBEKAH SACK

SO YOU WANT TO WRITE A CHILDREN'S BOOK: A STEP-BY-STEP GUIDE TO WRITING AND PUBLISHING FOR KIDS

1405 SW 6th Avenue • Ocala, Florida 34471 • Phone 800-814-1132 • Fax 352-622-1875
Website: www.atlantic-pub.com • Email: sales@atlantic-pub.com
SAN Number: 268-1250

Library of Congress Cataloging-in-Publication Data

Names: Sack, Rebekah, 1994- author.
Title: So you want to write a children's book : a step-by-step guide to
  writing and publishing for kids / by Rebekah Sack.
Description: Ocala, Florida : Atlantic Publishing Group, Inc., [2016] |
  Includes bibliographical references and index.
Identifiers: LCCN 2016035447| ISBN 9781620232132 (alk. paper) | ISBN
  1620232138 (alk. paper) | ISBN 9781620232293 (library binding : alk. paper)
Subjects: LCSH: Children's literature--Authorship--Juvenile literature. |
  Children's literature--Authorship--Marketing--Juvenile literature.
Classification: LCC PN147.5 .S15 2016 | DDC 808.06/8--dc23 LC record available at https://
lccn.loc.gov/2016035447

Printed in the United States

PROJECT MANAGER: Rebekah Sack • rsack@atlantic-pub.com
ASSISTANT EDITOR: Taylor Centers • gtcenters@gmail.com
INTERIOR LAYOUT AND JACKET DESIGN: Nicole Sturk • nicolejonessturk@gmail.com
COVER DESIGN: Jackie Miller • millerjackiej@gmail.com

Reduce. Reuse.
RECYCLE.

A decade ago, Atlantic Publishing signed the Green Press Initiative. These guidelines promote environmentally friendly practices, such as using recycled stock and vegetable-based inks, avoiding waste, choosing energy-efficient resources, and promoting a no-pulping policy. We now use 100-percent recycled stock on all our books. The results: in one year, switching to post-consumer recycled stock saved 24 mature trees, 5,000 gallons of water, the equivalent of the total energy used for one home in a year, and the equivalent of the greenhouse gases from one car driven for a year.

Over the years, we have adopted a number of dogs from rescues and shelters. First there was Bear and after he passed, Ginger and Scout. Now, we have Kira, another rescue. They have brought immense joy and love not just into our lives, but into the lives of all who met them.

We want you to know a portion of the profits of this book will be donated in Bear, Ginger and Scout's memory to local animal shelters, parks, conservation organizations, and other individuals and nonprofit organizations in need of assistance.

– Douglas & Sherri Brown,
President & Vice-President of Atlantic Publishing

Table of Contents

Foreword

A young friend of mine suffered terribly with night terrors, her fear of the dark so intense that even the simplest of pleasures, like going to a movie or camping under the stars, were terrifying prospects. No words could be found to alleviate her fears, because to her, the dark was an unsafe place, void of beauty and mystery. I started to think about the dark and what it meant to me. Yes, it could be scary, but what about all those things made more beautiful in the absence of light, all the life that exists beyond our sight and how busy and colorful the night truly is? That was the dark I wanted my young friend to see.

The idea for my children's book about the night began to emerge, and the tools at hand—my camera and Photoshop—became the method of illuminating my vision. The imagery came before the text, but it was the reading and research that helped shape the illustrations for my book. In some instances, like Moonbows, it was a new discovery. Really? Moonbows exist? I had to create that, even if it was just for me. What led to one curious discovery led to another, and another, and now there is a book called *OH! The Things You Can See In The Dark!*.

It took over eight years to complete the book—life gets in the way of life sometimes—yet it became, and continues to be, a wonderful journey of education and discovery, sometimes even a quiet retreat taking me out of my own personal darkness.

Suggestions for an aspiring young adult author? Keep writing, reading, listening and exploring—they are all keys to opening doors of your imagination. Take advantage of this book that offers you a tried and true foundation yet encourages you to think outside of the box.

My young friend? She has since grown up and is now a thespian performing on stage while we, the captivated audience, watch in the dark.

—Cathleen Francisco, debut children's author

Cathleen is a wine educator, photographer and author of two books on wine. OH! The Things You Can See In The Dark! is her first children's book, and she is currently working on a second book that continues the exploration into the night.

Living and working in Sonoma, Cathleen enjoys hikes and vineyard walks (camera always in hand) with her dog Belle. Visit her online at **www.catfrancisco.com**.

CHAPTER 1
Why Write for Kids?

I f you picked up this book, odds are you're a writer of some sort. You love the power of the written word, and you're interested in doing something tangible with your gift. That's pretty awesome if you ask us.

But (there's always a but, isn't there?), maybe you're not so sure about children's books. Maybe your dream is to write the next best fantasy book or maybe even the next *Infinite Jest*. If so, props to you for even considering it.

The big question is: Why write for kids? What does this area of expertise have to offer you as an aspiring author? Insert superhero music here—we have tons of reasons!

The Silver Screen Loves Children's Books

Hollywood gobbles up children's books like no other. Some of the most popular movies ever have been adapted from children's books. Here are some examples:

- *Charlotte's Web*
- *The Lorax*
- *Where the Wild Things Are*
- *Diary of a Wimpy Kid*
- *The Chronicles of Narnia*
- *James and the Giant Peach*
- *Charlie and the Chocolate Factory*
- *Mary Poppins*
- *How the Grinch Stole Christmas*
- *101 Dalmatians*
- *Alice in Wonderland*

- *Winnie the Pooh*

- *The Jungle Book*

- ...the list goes on!

If your children's book ends up being a showstopper, you might be able to option it for film — and we all know what that means. Money. (And fame.)

Kids Read More Than Adults

The chances that your book will fall into the lap of a child aren't actually so bad. Kids read more than adults. It doesn't take a rocket scientist to realize this, either. The books are shorter, and reading is often part of a child's bedtime routine.

Reading for pleasure peaks in the fifth grade — it's kind of sad for adults, but it's good news for you. This area is constantly growing, and libraries are always stocking up on new children's books.

You Might Be Able to Scrape Up A Living

Children's books sell well, because everyone is buying them. Not only are parents buying them for their kids, but libraries and schools are getting in on the action, too. When children's books win awards or are featured somewhere, schools and libraries start placing bulk orders, which means more money in your pocket.

If you find that you have a serious talent in this area, you might be one of those writers that don't have to work a second job.

You Can Be Weird

Have you seen the stuff going on in kid's books? You can write anything you want, and no one cares, because you're writing a children's book. Suddenly, all bets are off.

Gravity doesn't exist? It's cool.

Everyone has twelve arms? No problem.

You poop rainbows? No one blinks an eye.

You can write anything your heart desires, and kids will probably just think it's cool.

You'll Become a Word Master

Children are tough critics. If every aspect of a book doesn't keep their attention and excite them, they're not going to stand for it. Back on the shelf it goes. For that reason, you have to make sure every single element of your book is spot on.

From wording and rhythm to illustrations and character development, kids are expecting to be delighted. You have to nail it. When an older audience opens a children's book, we sometimes think, "Geez, anyone could write that. 'No more monkeys jumping on the bed?' Easy as pie."

The thing is, sometimes we think that more is . . . better. But, when it comes to children's books, less is definitely more. The simpler, the better. And that can be hard.

Why is this a good thing, you're asking? If you're serious about writing, you can become an amazing writer through this experience. You'll appreciate everything that comes along with telling a story, because you'll have challenged yourself. It all comes together when you learn to write for a younger audience.

In other words, you'll become a word master.

The Fan Mail Rocks

Nothing is better than getting fan mail from kids. They're so honest and sweet — their notes are usually hand-written, too. Maybe they sprinkle in some original artwork. Either way, knowing that you've inspired a kid is pretty awesome.

There are a lot of other things that are rewarding when it comes to writing children's books (you're effectively impacting a child's development), but hopefully these reasons are enough to get you on the bandwagon.

Let's move forward and take a look at the different types of children's books. While reading this next chapter, try to hone in on which age group interests you most.

CHAPTER 2
Types of Children's Books

I f you want to write it, you need to read it.

This tidbit of advice is true for anyone in any profession. Think of musicians—jazz musicians are very well versed (pun intended) in the history of jazz, because it's important that they know what came before them. You better believe that they know all about Billie Holiday, Miles Davis, Charlie Parker, and Louis Armstrong. The same goes for any other profession. Any educated architect will know all about Michelangelo and Frank Lloyd Wright.

Not only do people need to know what came before them, but they can take inspiration from those in their field. This is especially true for artists. Without Van Gogh, who knows where the art movement would've gone?

In the case of writing, it's important to know what kinds of books are in your area of expertise so that you aren't doubling what's already out there (among lots of other reasons). Themes and topics can be reused time and time again, but if your title is the same as someone else's, people will know that you haven't done your homework.

So, check out the competition and spend a good deal of time in the children's and young adult sections of the library or bookstore. Try to understand what is being written, as well as what works and what doesn't. Every writer should also be a reader—after all, reading and writing go hand in hand. Know what's out there and stay on top of trends, current issues, what kids are reading, and what they're putting back on the shelf.

Baby Books (0 to 15 months)

Baby books have become increasingly common in recent years, as educators, reading experts, and parents have come to stand by the belief that the earlier you read to kids, the better. We now know that, while *in utero*, infants can hear the mother's voice and the voices of those around her.

Examples:

- *Gossie & Gertie* by Oliver Dunrae

- *Where is Baby's Belly Button?* by Karen Katz

- *Goodnight Moon* by Margaret Wise Brown

Baby books can be formatted as picture books, board books, or books made from other materials, such as cloth or plastic designed for the teething set. Some baby books contain noisemakers, various fabrics, textile materials (touch-and-feel books), crinkly materials, and other features designed to appeal to the senses.

Manuscripts for baby books are often around 250 words, or close to a full or half typewritten page in length. Some manuscripts, such as those containing nursery rhymes or lullabies, can run longer. A typical baby book in print may be 8 to 12 pages in length.

Board Books (1 to 3 years)

Board books are the 6 to 16 page chunky books printed on cardboard and built to withstand the wrath of a child's hands. They range everywhere from simple stories and lift-the-flap books to condensed classics and stories already printed in picture-book format. They may contain a basic storyline or simply deal with concepts such as shapes, numbers, and colors.

Examples:

- *Chicka Chicka ABC* by John Archambault and Bill Martin, Jr.

- *The Very Hungry Caterpillar* by Eric Carle

- *How Do Dinosaurs Say Goodnight?* by Jane Yolen

Most board books are created either from an existing picture book, are written in-house, or are created by an illustrator. Because of this, opportunities for children's authors are limited in this category. Many stories appear in picture book format before crossing over to new life as a board book.

Picture Books (2 to 7; 7 to 12 years)

As the name suggests, picture books are heavily illustrated with full-color, eye-catching pictures, and they're printed in 16, 24, 32, 40, or 48 pages, with 32 pages being the most common length. Most books are published with such specific page numbers because they are bound in "signatures," or groups of folded pages numbering 8 or 16. These are sewn together in a binding.

Characters in picture books are capable of overcoming the most challenging obstacles, they face real-life issues, and they perform heroic acts. Picture books also cover simple stories with basic plots, concepts such as counting and shapes, and subjects that are familiar and comforting to children.

Keep in mind that children do not like to be condescended to. Nonfiction picture books geared for toddlers can be quite different from those intended for 7-year-olds. Books aimed at younger children may, at the simplest levels, identify concepts, animals, or objects, for example. Older children like more details and specific information. Children falling in the middle of the age group, such as a 5-year-olds, still enjoy illustrations and like details, but none that are too lengthy or complex.

Examples:

- *Uncle Andy's* by James Warhola

- *Winter Lullaby* by Barbara Seuling

- *If I Only Had a Horn: Young Louis Armstrong* by Roxane Orgill

Picture books designed for older children are targeted toward readers who are ages 7 to 12. Often with elaborate layouts and strong overall visual components, these books are complemented with illustrations, paintings, photographs, and collages. The reading level is more sophisticated to match that of older readers, and subjects are presented informatively on topics such as history, art, and science, to name a few.

Examples:

- *Click, Clack, Moo: Cows that Type* by Betsy Lewin

- *The Great Pig Search* by Eileen Christelow

- *Leonardo da Vinci* by Diane Stanley

- *Prairie Dogs Kiss and Lobsters Wave: How Animals Say Hello* by Marilyn Singer

Easy-to-Read Books (5 to 7 years)

Easy-to-read books can appear in picture book or chapter book format, but are presented so they seem more mature to beginning readers. They are available in fiction and nonfiction in a wide variety of subjects, and often appear as a series geared toward different reading levels.

Examples:

- Simon & Schuster's *Ready-to-Read* books

- Dr. Seuss books

These books are illustrated for added interest, but illustrations are smaller and less prominent than in picture books. For the purposes of easier reading, more white space appears per page than in chapter books for older children, with the leading (the space between lines; pronounced *led-ing*) increased as well. Easy-to-read picture books are typically around 32 pages, and easy-to-read chapter books can range from 48 to 64 pages. These books can be anywhere from a few hundred words to around 1,500.

Hopeful writers of easy-to-read books should keep in mind that, because easy readers most often appear in a series, they will need to seek publishers who are interested in publishing new series titles. Beginning or unpublished writers pitching series ideas rarely experience success; it is better to wait until you have more publications under your belt or to offer up a stand-alone title.

Early Chapter Books (7 to 10 years)

Early chapter books are a precursor to middle grade books. They are often illustrated, but the text predominates. Chapter books traditionally refer to books divided into chapters, but also to books that are more advanced than early readers and contain stories and sentences that are somewhat more developed and complex. While plots are more advanced than those of easy-to-read books, they are kept relatively simple and easy to understand, with short chapters, large type, and plenty of white space (which translates into wide leading and sometimes, generous margins).

Examples:

- *Captain Underpants* by Dav Pilkey
- *The Kids of the Polk Street School* by Patricia Reilly Giff
- *Spider Storch's Fumbled Field Trip* by Gina Willner-Pardo

Some chapter books resolve a conflict, episode, or subplot by the end of each chapter, while others leave the reader wanting to know more at chapter's end. With humor and plenty of dialogue and action, these books range from 48 pages to more than 100 pages in length. Chapter book manuscripts typically run 6 to 40 pages, or 1,500 to 10,000 words.

Middle Grade Books (8 to 12 years)

What do readers ages 8 to 12 like to read? Most children falling into this category look for fantasy, adventure, humor, horror, and family-oriented stories and sagas. These young adventure-seekers enjoy action and solid storytelling, replete with tension and events that logically develop.

Most middle grade fiction books are comprised of 8 to 16 chapters, and include more subplots, character development, and greater detail about the subject, setting, events, and characters than books for earlier ages. Most manuscripts in this category contain 10,000 to 30,000 words and span from 40 to 120 pages. Printed fiction usually runs from 48 to 200 pages, and sometimes longer. Young middle grade fiction (8 to 9 years old) usually weighs in from 48 to 80 pages; true middle grade books (8 to 12 years) about 80 to 160 pages; and older middle grade or young adult transitional (10 to 14 years) from 128 to more than 200 pages. Nonfiction in print commonly ranges from 64 to 100 pages in length.

Examples of middle grade fiction:

- *Julie of the Wolves* by Jean Craighead George

- *Hoot* by Carl Hiaasen

- *James and the Giant Peach* by Roald Dahl

- *Charlotte's Web* by E. B. White

- J. K. Rowling's *Harry Potter* series

Children in this age group are also developing their first sense of what literature is and may form devotions to certain authors, whom they often remember fondly for years to come. Writers for this genre of children's literature are writing for a more sophisticated audience who will notice weaknesses in plot and flaws in logic, but who also appreciate more twists and turns in plot and well-rounded, realistic characters to whom they can relate.

Examples of middle grade nonfiction:

- *The Scholastic Dictionary of Idioms* by Marvin Terban

- *Once a Wolf: How Biologists Fought to Bring Back the Gray Wolf* by Stephen R. Swinburne

- *Auschwitz: The Story of a Nazi Death Camp* by Clive A. Lawton

Young Adult (12 years and up)

In keeping with the trend of increasing complexity and level of detail, young adult novels are geared for readers ages 12 and up, whose understanding of the world and reading level is rapidly increasing. The lives of these young readers are often socially and family-oriented, and they like to read books that deal with complex relationships. Their fiction addresses more in the way of emotion, value assessments, unusual or difficult situations and behaviors, and introspection. Often, the books written for these truth-seekers are humorous, quirky, realistic, or emotional.

Writers for this age group use more flashbacks and other complex methods of storytelling, such as alternating points of view or shifting between characters. Readers of young adult fiction want to be able to identify with the characters, who are sometimes faced with seemingly impossible situations, and often deal with such themes as death, love, fear, peer pressure, addiction, independence, relationships, pregnancy, proving themselves, and many more similar subjects. These types of books are often genre-oriented.

Examples of young adult fiction:

- The *Divergent* trilogy by Veronica Roth

- *The Fault in Our Stars* by John Green

- *The Hunger Games* trilogy by Suzanne Collins

Young adult nonfiction covers nearly all subjects and targets the knowledge seeker. Some of the most popular among the young adult readership are books that still relate to them on their level. Ideas are more advanced and often ask probing questions younger readers may not be ready for in areas such as politics, art, religion, technology, and war. Young adult sections in bookstores are expanding.

Examples of young adult nonfiction:

- *Runaway Girl: The Artist Louise Bourgeois* by Jan Greenberg and Sandra Jordan

- The *Rookie* Yearbooks by Tavi Gevinson

- *Go: A Kidd's Guide to Graphic Design* by Chip Kidd

Manuscripts are usually from 120 to 225 pages long, and can run anywhere from 30,000 to 56,000 words; printed books are commonly 168 to 300 pages long. Lengths vary from house to house, however, and writers should check publisher guidelines before submitting work in this genre.

Children's Graphic Novels

Graphic novels for children are an exciting, up-and-coming genre that tends to contain stories of increased complexity as opposed to their comic book cousins. Graphic novels are common abroad, especially in France and Belgium. Similar editions of these in Japan are called manga, or comics.

Major publishing houses in the United States now approach graphic novels with the same level of care and pride afforded to picture books and other children's literature. While publishers are beginning to catch on to this trend in children's literature, the field is still new and developing, which is tremendously exciting for writers.

Children's graphic novels are formatted in a fashion similar to comic books, and text and illustrations often work hand in hand to tell the story. Graphic novels are sometimes thought of as interchangeable with comic books, but there are a few key differences. Whereas a comic book is often part of a series, in which a single comic book contains an episode, a graphic novel consists of a complete story, from beginning to end.

Sometimes, however, an entire series of comics is published as a collection—but it is still a comic collection and not a graphic novel.

Another difference lies in the fact that graphic novels, like traditional novels, are given ISBNs, whereas comic books are issued with ISSNs, a number that is given to magazines and journals.

Printed graphic novels are typically a little more than 100 pages long, but are sometimes as short as 32 pages or as long as 400+ pages. With editions in hardcover and paperback, what are known as "trade comics" can come in three primary forms: collections of comic strips (such as *Garfield* or *Calvin and Hobbes*); trade paperbacks, which are novel versions of stories originally published in a comic book format; or graphic novels, which can constitute a full-length collection of stories or a single, novel-length story.

Examples:

- *March: Book One* by John Lewis and Andrew Aydin; illustrated by Nate Powell

- *Bow Wow*, by Megan Montague Cash; illustrated by Mark Newgarden

- *American Born Chinese* by Gene Luen Yang

- *The Plain Janes* by Cecil Castellucci and Jim Rugg

- *The Adventures of Super Diaper Baby: The First Graphic Novel* by Dav Pilkey

- *Doraemon* by Fujiko Fujio

- *Fushigi Yûgi* by Yuu Watase

- *Arizona* by Mac McCool

Plays

Plays for adult performers to a children's audience are abundant; however, there is a need for more plays written for children to watch *and* perform. Beyond the traditional seasonal fare performed across the country in many churches and schools, plays for children are an overlooked or sometimes under-encouraged market. For this reason, if you are a playwright, your best bet is to read published plays and collections, and investigate who is publishing them. As with all submissions, be sure to thoroughly look into each individual publisher's guidelines before submitting.

Examples:

- *Small Plays for Special Days* by Sue Alexander

- *Winterthing: A Play for Children* by Joan Aiken and John Sebastian Brown

- *Ten Plays for Children: From the Repertory of the Children's Theatre Company of Minneapolis* by Timothy Mason

- *Theater for Young Audiences: 20 Great Plays for Children* edited by Coleman Jennings

Poetry

Beyond the usual rhyming fare found in picture books, poetry as stand-alone work for children is available for all age groups. Children love the sing-song lilt and rhythm of poetry. Writing poetry is a difficult and very particular art form that demands from its writer a certain economy of language and sensibility for fine-tuning words, form, and ideas. Every word must be right; every syllable must be purposeful.

Poetry particularly appeals to children because of its length and can benefit reluctant or struggling readers. Publishers tend to be picky about poetry. Some love rhyme, while others will not tolerate it. Because so many editors have read their fair share of poetry that rhymes simply for the sake of rhyming, and does so while losing meaning—whether in character development, plot, setting, or description—some don't consider poetry or manuscripts containing rhyme for publication.

Examples:

- *Where the Sidewalk Ends* by Shel Silverstein

- *Exploding Gravy: Poems to Make You Laugh* by X. J. Kennedy

- *Revolting Rhymes* by Roald Dahl

- *Hailstones and Halibut Bones* written by Mary O'Neill; illustrated by John Wallner

- *Paint Me Like I Am: Teen Poems* from WritersCorps by Bill Aguado and Richard Newirth

Now that you have a general idea of your options, try to focus on one idea to begin with. Which area interests you most? Which genre do you think you'd excel at? Give yourself some time to read through some examples—use the ones we've provided for you as a starting place—and try to imagine writing your own book.

To take a step away from the creative process for a moment, let's take a sneak peek into the publishing industry. If you're a writer, you need to understand the business side of it all.

CHAPTER 3

Getting to Know the Publishing Industry

W riting can be an awesome creative outlet, but you can't exactly do whatever you want—unless you don't care about being published. The publishing industry is an industry after all, and the goal is to make money, so if your book doesn't look like it'll do the job, you'll get the boot.

So, before you get knee deep into your first children's book, it's worthwhile to get to know the publishing industry to make sure you're on the right track. We'll be looking at the basic structure of a publishing company as well as the different types of publishers.

Different Parts of a Publishing Company

There is a huge concentration of publishing companies in New York City—if you're a writer, you probably know this and have considered moving there for this reason.

The publishing industry has lately become more corporate, at least where the larger houses are concerned. Publishing houses have recently

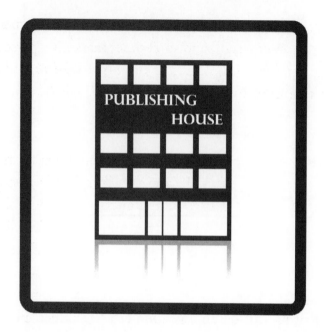

undergone mergers and acquisitions with larger-scale companies. From the 1980s to the present day, publishers have started pairing up, making them take over the world of publishing. These pairings are commonly known as the *megapublishers*.

What this means for you is that you'll potentially have more opportunities for licensing your product. If the contract allows, a licensing agreement will provide for the publisher to sell the idea to other companies, potentially resulting in offshoots of characters and story. The main character may become a doll, game, television show, or movie. That means more money in your pocket.

Imprints

Larger publishers have what are known as "imprints." An imprint is a specialized subdivision of a publishing house that focuses on a certain area and often carries a certain identity. An imprint is sometimes named after its editor (such as Joanna Cotler Books at HarperCollins), and employs editorial staff, and sometimes marketing personnel who are particular to that imprint. The *Children's Writer's & Illustrator's Market* lists imprints by publisher.

Divisions

A division is often a group of imprints in a house that form a department, such as the children's division. The Random House children's publishing division is comprised of 22 imprints and publishing lines, including Alfred A. Knopf Books for Young Readers, Yearling Books, and Bantam Books. The Knopf imprint produces hardcover editions and is quality-focused; Yearling Books are paperback editions targeted for children ages 8 to 12; and Bantam Books are commercial paperbacks with an angle on movie and television material and original series.

Lines

A line is part of an imprint, and may include easy-to-read books. One example of a line is *Step into Reading* from Random House, whose publications include books that increase a child's reading abilities according to different levels of difficulty. A series, on the other hand, can be part of a line.

Series examples:

- The Junie B. Jones books by Barbara Park
- The Magic Tree House Series by Mary Hope Osborne

Books in a series come out with new titles once a month or several times per year. A group of series can comprise a line, and several lines can fall under one imprint.

Types of Publishers

Publishers come in all shapes and sizes. The field of children's publishing is super diverse, especially because there are so many different types of children's books out there. Not all publishers are created equally — before submitting anything, always read through the publisher's guidelines.

While some publishers accept unsolicited (un-agented) manuscripts and queries, many more, especially in the larger houses, don't. The recent mergers and acquisitions mentioned earlier have resulted in large publishing houses becoming even larger, but their hallowed halls are still not completely inaccessible. Read on for an overview of the different types of publishing markets.

Trade publishers

Trade publishing houses often range in size. These publishers produce high-quality, often hardcover, and more expensive books, which they sell to schools, bookstores, and libraries. With a concentration in New York City, these publishers are among the largest of the publishers in staff size and budget. They commonly offer royalties and advances to authors, and seek quality and originality in the manuscripts they review. Trade publishing houses contain smaller divisions, or imprints, which are managed independently of each other and have different editorial staff. Trade publications tend to receive the most and highest-profile reviews.

Large houses have the biggest budgets. A house is considered "large" when annual sales are more than $50 million. They publish and promote more than 500 books per year and their authors receive the highest standard in the industry of marketing, publicity, and promotion. They also review the largest volume of manuscripts, and this is

where the competition is also the strongest. Authors have a higher chance of a large publishing house accepting their manuscript when they take the time to research and evaluate the writing competition, different publishers, and the needs and output of specific houses.

Medium-sized or moderate houses typically bring in between $10 million and $50 million in annual sales and publish more than 100 books every year. While these publishers are not the corporate giants that large houses often are, companies vary widely and range from newspaper chains to private businesses that are managed by a single person. Still others are managed and run as though they are large, successful family operations.

Knopf Trade Paperbacks is an imprint of Random House whose paperbacks are targeted toward middle grade and young adult readers. In stark contrast to the corporate giant, Random House, an example of a medium-sized children's trade publisher is Roaring Brook Press, a children's imprint of Macmillan.

Small and independent presses

Small presses, small publishers, and independent presses and publishers are a type of trade publisher who sell through mail order and sometimes directly or indirectly to the same outlets as large and medium trade publishers. While their budgets are smaller than those of larger houses, with annual sales under $10 million, they offer benefits in several areas.

Small presses often market to specialized audiences, such as readers of poetry, for example, and will often keep a title in print for longer than a larger house would. Small publishers may offer royalties and advances, royalties with no advance, or may simply pay in contributor copies (the author is provided copies of his or her books in lieu of monetary payment).

Small and independent presses are often attractive to authors whose work may fall into a niche market or specialty category. Small presses also tend to be somewhat more approachable than larger houses and accept higher rates of unsolicited manuscripts.

Also, these houses frequently provide the breakthrough into the market for first-time authors and illustrators, allowing for the opportunity to establish new careers. If you don't want to submit your book to a huge corporation or if your book isn't easily marketable, you might consider a small, independent press.

Mass market

Mass-market publications are the typically less-expensive paperback versions of books published by trade publishers. These publications are marketed to the masses and often host well-known characters, spin-off characters, series books, and popular media tie-ins, such as books based on movies, television shows, and websites. While still available at large chain bookstores, mass-market paperbacks are most

commonly found in supermarkets and budget retail stores, and in newsstands and airport shops. They often reach these markets via independent distributors.

Mass-market publishers sometimes hire ghostwriters or freelance writers to produce series books; illustrators are similarly limited in their range of possible creativity when they are hired to reproduce pre-existing characters for books, such as those from popular movies and television shows. Mass-market books are not as widely reviewed as trade publications but can reach widespread levels of distribution.

Some examples of mass-market books are:

- The Dell Laurel-Leaf edition of *Bud, Not Buddy* by Christopher Paul Curtis

- *Civil War on Sunday* by Mary Pope Osborne, No. 21 in the Magic Tree House Series

CASE STUDY: SUZANNE LIEURANCE

Author, Freelance Writer, The Working
Writer's Coach
Jensen Beach, Florida, USA

Working on assignments for mass-market publishers can be both fun and challenging. The trick is to gain entrance into their stable of regular writers. It's often tricky because you won't always find mass-market publishers listed in writers' market guides. And, if these publishers have websites, there are usually no guidelines for writers at their sites, either.

So, here's what I suggest you do if you're interested in writing for mass-market publishers but can't find any information about them. Go to large supermarket chains or even to a big bookstore and look for the children's books. Among the children's books, look for big books that are actually anthologies (collections of stories written by different authors). Next, look in the front of each book or anthology to find the name and address of the publisher. More than likely, the publisher will be a company you've never heard of. That's good, though, because it usually means this is a mass market publisher. Also, look for a website address (the URL) for each publisher and check out their website.

Look around for writers' guidelines (often referred to as submissions guidelines). Sometimes, this information can be found on the **contact** page for the publisher or the **about** page. If you can't find any writers' or submissions guidelines, look for any contact information. The name of an acquisitions editor would be perfect, but often that information isn't at the site either. Not to worry. Simply get the mailing address for the publisher and the phone number. Next, call the publisher and ask for the name of their acquisitions editor or submissions editor (they may have several, so just get the name of one of them).

Write a personalized cover letter that:

- Introduces you to the editor
- Explains that you would like to work for the company on an assignment
- Says that your resume is enclosed for review
- Encourages the editor to keep your resume on file should any work become available

You might even include a few appropriate writing samples (meaning samples like the type of stories and other materials this publisher publishes), and then send off your packet to this editor.

Next, prepare to wait. You may not ever hear from this editor or publisher. But, if your cover letter is engaging and your resume shows that you know something about writing for children, you will probably hear from the publisher when you least expect it. They **finally** have a project that is right for you.

It took almost a year from the time I submitted a packet to a mass-market publisher before I heard from them with an assignment. But, once I completed that first assignment satisfactorily and on time (this is really important), I worked for them regularly for many years, and I was given all sorts of interesting (and often challenging) projects.

You'll learn a lot by writing for mass-market publishers, because they have very strict guidelines. For example, one of my first assignments for a mass-market publisher was to read the original version of *The Three Musketeers* (written by Alexander Dumas for adults; it was almost 400 pages) then rewrite (adapt) this story for children (ages 8-12) in just 12 pages of 250 words per page. Another time, this publisher sent me 10 pieces of artwork (it came from a poem they had printed years ago in another book). My assignment was to use this artwork to create a new story in 10 pages (one picture per page, and I had to use every picture), in no more than 150 words per page.

If you like challenges, writing for mass market publishers might be the way to start your career as a children's writer. I suggest you give it a try and find out. Have fun!

*Suzanne Lieurance is the author of over 30 published books (mostly children's books). She is a former classroom teacher, and she was an instructor for the Institute of Children's Literature for over eight years. As director of the Working Writer's Club (**www.workingwritersclub.com**) and a writing coach, she specializes in helping people turn their passion for writing into a career. For free writing tips and other resources, subscribe to The Morning Nudge at **www.morningnudge.com**.*

E-publishers

E-publishers are often small presses publishing in traditional print and online formats, or in electronic format only. They produce previously unpublished work, or reproduce works that are currently in print or that have fallen out of print. Some e-publishers offer print-on-demand (POD) options, so users can print a hardcopy version.

Due to the wide variety of e-publishers and the low production costs involved in e- publishing, you might find that this is a great option for you. Keep in mind, though, that you won't necessary get the benefits of sales, marketing, and prestige that you might get from a traditional publisher.

Until handheld electronic reading devices like Amazon's Kindle become a staple in every home, children's books will be most popular in print form. However, as much as the benefits of electronic literature are clear, young children have always been and will always be tactile creatures that experience pleasure from holding a book, turning the pages, and looking at the glossy illustrations.

Educational publishers

Educational publishers are part of what is known as the institutional market, which sells its products to libraries, schools, and educational distributors. Children's educational publishers produce encyclopedias, nonfiction, general textbooks, home school materials, and other academic publications.

Institutional publishers also produce book series more commonly than trade publishers. For authors seeking to publish work in the

children's institutional market, it is necessary to be familiar with the educational curriculum for the targeted age group. Educational publishers typically offer a flat fee or royalties with little to no advance. Large publishers such as Houghton Mifflin and Macmillan/McGraw-Hill publish textbooks and supplementary materials, as do smaller houses specializing in educational publications.

Religious publishers

Publishers of religious books and materials focus on one or more religions, topics, or themes and sell their product to specialized markets, such as religious bookstores and churches, or to bookstores with religious and inspirational sections. Like educational publishers, religious publishers usually provide a flat fee or royalties with little to no advance to their authors. These publishers are highly specialized and typically offer books of prayer or traditional verse geared toward a particular religious belief system, as well as fiction, nonfiction, and poetry concerning specific morals and values.

Book packagers

Somewhere between publishers and writers, there are book packagers. Book packagers bring publishers' ideas and projects to life, and sometimes bring their own ideas and projects to publishers. Packagers handle writing, editing, illustration, and book design for a single book or a series. The publisher then receives the package and sends it off for printing and distribution. Book packagers contract with illustrators and writers for their content and are always seeking talent.

Here are some general characteristics of book packagers:

- They usually give you an outline of the story they want you to write

- The plot is already chosen—you just have to write the story

- Deadlines are very tight

- You are usually paid a flat fee for your writing

- You must be able to collaborate

- You usually don't have your actual name on the cover—you write under a collective pseudonym

Here are some examples of books that are products of book packaging:

- *The Vampire Diaries* series by L. J. Smith

- The *Gossip Girl* series by Cecily von Ziegesar

- The *Nancy Drew* series by Carolyn Keene

Some authors and illustrators find this type of work a good way to break into the industry, hone their skills, and learn how to work with editors and other publishing professionals. Writers and illustrators for book packagers are subcontracted under work-for-hire contracts, in which they receive a flat fee and limited or no royalties. The author is considered a ghostwriter. Book packagers produce many children's and young adult series books, such as romance and adventure books.

In the end, you can choose whichever kind of publisher you want—you might get steered in a certain direction based on what kind of book you want to write. If you're writing for the masses, you can consider submitting to a larger press. If you want to start small, you might consider going with a local or small-business owner publisher.

If you want to get some practice in the publishing world, you might actually consider trying out a book packager.

Just knowing your options is an awesome first step to becoming a children's book writer. Now that you have a general idea of what to expect in the industry, it's time to start writing. The next chapter will give you the basics on how to write for kids.

CHAPTER 4

Writing for Kids: The Basics

You already know how important it is to actually read children's books if you want to write them. Don't be shy—you might get strange looks when you're reading *The Giving Tree* on the bus, but know that you're immersing yourself in your craft. We can give you the basics, but like anything else, learning from experience is going to help you more than anything else.

Regardless of this fact, we're still going to try to help you understand the basics of writing for kids. This chapter is going to focus on what children like to read, choosing a topic for your first book, how to effectively brainstorm, and more.

Let's get started.

What Children Like to Read

Writing to appeal to a wide audience should be your goal, because it's part of what editors and publishers look for in a manuscript. Remember that publishing is a business, and the bottom line of a

business is almost always money. Publishers want what will sell, and what sells is usually what kids like to read—but that's kind of the challenge. What gives your work that extra spark that sets it apart from others in its genre? How can you make your book speak to kids *and* the publisher?

In order to truly connect with our audience, it helps to see things from a kid's point of view. That means more than just remembering what it was like to be 7 or 12 years old. Our memories change so much, and with our growing maturity, it becomes impossible to truly remember what it was like to be so young. Basically, you need to go a step further.

It means noticing children when you're out, playing with children when you can, noticing their reactions to specific books. It means paying attention to the way children talk, to the way they react to certain situations, to the way they look at the world.

CASE STUDY: FIONA TAPP

CLASSIFIED CASE STUDIES
directly from the experts

Freelance Writer and Educator
Ontario, Canada

After over 13 years as a classroom teacher, I have read thousands of books to children. Because of this, I have a keen sense of what holds their attention, what challenges them, and what totally entrenches them with magic.

Many of the stories that have been class favorites over the years share similar qualities. They are told with a rhythmic quality that, if not actually containing rhymes, at least sound pleasing to the ear when read aloud. They often have an element of the silly or absurd (humor plays an important role) and a strong hero who has to battle a formidable enemy or overcome a personal struggle. Successful children's authors speak especially and directly to children and never patronize or talk down to them. The main characters in many famous children's books are other children so that young readers can see themselves in the story.

As a writer myself, I think the most important thing you can do when drafting your story is to read it aloud. This helps you check for grammar problems, nuance, and style, and it lets you listen to the tone and rhythmic quality of your work. You might feel silly reading aloud, so go somewhere private and practice in front of the mirror, or record yourself and watch it back. Once you have something you are proud of, read it to a group of children and ask for their honest opinions (which are the only opinions young children seem able to offer!). Ask them which parts make them laugh, which parts scare or surprise them, ask if they like the main characters, and ask if they would like to see anything else in the story. It can be hard to ask for feedback — it can knock your ego to hear negative things about your creation, and after working so long on a creative endeavor, you have to be brave to share it, and you must be open to constructive criticism. This step is necessary if you want your story to improve and if you want to become a professional writer. Many critically acclaimed authors didn't find their creative voice until they were over 40, so if you already know you're a writer, you're ahead of the game. Work on perfecting your method to release the wealth of stories you have inside — good luck!

Fiona Tapp is a freelance writer and educator, an expert in Pedagogy, and a Master's Degree holder in Education. Originally from England, she now lives in Canada. She writes about a variety of topics including parenting, education, and travel, as well as feminist perspectives and personal opinion pieces. She can be found at **www.fionatapp.com** *or* **www.lullabiesanddeadlines.com.**

You want your dialogue to be realistic, and you want your characters to be memorable and convincing. In order to do this, you *must* interact with children. Listen to how they narrate an event, and consider their methods of storytelling when you are writing. If this doesn't come organically, just ask a child that you know to tell you a story. For example, "How did you meet your best friend?" Listen to where they begin, how fast they speak, and the kinds of words they use. If you need to, record it so that you can listen to it later.

Young readers are more sophisticated than many adults give them credit for, and they will spot a mouthpiece a mile away. Adult perspectives speaking through young characters almost always come off as preachy and unconvincing, and as a result, they don't tend to do well in the marketplace.

Many writers figure out how to walk the line between showing good morals and coming off as preachy by letting the main character be very independent. You rarely see parents telling the main character what to do in a children's book—instead, the main character finds the resolution on her own, which appeals to both parents and children.

Children attend school to learn lessons, and they read books for entertainment and pleasure. If a book interests them, you've won the battle.

Choosing a Topic

When you are thinking about what to write, read books on the bestseller list to get a feel for what's selling and what publishers are spending money on to promote. Read reviews of as many children's books as you can find to discover what are considered strong points of current books and what are considered flaws and weaknesses. *Kirkus*

Reviews, *Publishers Weekly*, and *The Horn Book Magazine* are some sources of children's book reviews.

What topics does your local children's librarian feel is lacking on her shelves? Consider those topics for your next book. Publications like the bulletin published by the Society of Children's Book Writers and Illustrators (SCBWI) and industry magazines such as *Writer's Digest* sometimes provide topics that publishers and librarians would like to see written about by children's book authors.

Another important thing to consider is what the hot topics of the moment are. Politics can play a huge part in children's literature, especially if it's a topic that no one else is talking about. For example, many publishers are seeking children's books that have diverse characters, such as LGBT or Native American characters. There's suddenly a gap in the industry, and publishers are interested in filling it.

Whether you're writing to get published or you're writing for yourself, the most important thing to do is to choose a topic that speaks to you. If you aren't passionate about your topic, your book will fall to the bottom of the shelf.

Originality is the key to writing a dazzling manuscript. When you are brainstorming story ideas, ask yourself:

- Has this idea been written about many times before?

- If so, can I contribute anything new?

- What do I feel strongly about?

- What can I write about that is unique to my experience?

- What are my true passions?

- What has not been written about yet?

- What could I add to the topic that is unique? Perhaps a fresh way of telling the story or unique characterization is what will set such a story apart from the crowd.

To help you brainstorm, here's a list of the most popular themes with some sample topics taken from the Reading Rockets website (**www.readingrockets.org**).

- Friends and family
  - Best friends, fathers, a new marriage

- Social studies
  - Maps, real life heroines, biographies

- Genres
  - Poems, graphic novels, nursery rhymes, folktales

- Feelings
  - Being brave, love, favorite things

- Holidays
  - Thanksgiving, Halloween, Christmas

- Creatures
  - Bugs, dogs, sea creatures

- Interests
  - Art, music, national parks, princesses

- Events and special days
  - Hispanic Heritage Month, Black History Month, back to school

- Seasons
  - Books for the beach, snow, signs of spring

- Taking action
  - Freedom stories, heroes, making a difference

- Science and math
  - Aliens, how things work, counting

- Me and my life
  - School, teachers, tooth fairy

- Fun and funny
  - Field trips, gross things, jokes

- Reading and language arts
  - Rhyming, words, word sounds

- Nighty night
  - Bedtime stories

Topics to avoid

Methods of approaching different topics and ideas about what is and is not acceptable sometimes fluctuate in children's publishing. There are some constants, especially concerning picture books, where the subject matter should be appropriate for children ages 2 to 7 (or 3 to 8, depending on the publisher's guidelines and publication standards).

Here is a brief list of things to keep in mind:

- Topics where inanimate objects are the main characters aren't usually that successful—both children and editors seek characters with more life and substance.

- Overly sentimental topics rarely do well.

- It may be wise to avoid plots and formulas that have been

done too many times. Try to infuse your story with its own unique, original flavor.

- Avoid themes that are outlandish or gimmicky. Themes should emerge from the story naturally and not be forced; the worst a theme can be is moralistic and preachy.

Coming Up With Ideas

If you're totally new to this writing thing and don't even know where to begin, it can be really intimidating. Coming up with fresh ideas that are not only unique, but that you're also passionate about can be really challenging. To help ease the pain, we have several strategies you can use to develop those Nobel-winning ideas.

Write in a journal or notebook

Journal writing is a way to stimulate ideas without feeling pressured to come up with anything specific. Use a journal or notebook to write down your observations about the things, places, people, and events around you. You can also use the journal to determine your best time for writing.

Experiment by writing at different times so you can see when you are at your most inspired or productive — are you an early bird or a night owl? Writing in a journal allows you the pleasure of writing just for the sake of writing. There is no structure, limitation, or deadline involved. Try not to read or judge what you have written—ever.

Here are some ideas to get you journaling:

- Write about what is happening in your life at the time, specifically your thoughts and emotions.

- Write about your dreams when you wake up.

- Experiment with writing in different forms—don't force yourself to adhere to a specific structure.

- Could any of the objects around you be used in a story? Look for details like mis-buttoned jackets, different-colored socks, polished shoes, or perfectly knotted ties.

- Choose a different topic to write about every day.

- Go to the park, the mall, or any dedicated place to sit down and write about what you see.

- Try writing down whatever pieces of conversation you can decipher from the chatter around you.

Life experience

It is often said that truth is stranger than fiction. Real experiences can make for some of the most interesting storylines and sources of inspiration, especially when writing for children, who love plenty of action and adventurous situations.

Keep in mind that details of people, mood, events, and places can always be changed. If you are basing your story off of something that really happened to you, consider the areas that might do better with some fictional elements. Here are some examples:

- Real: Your friend accidentally trips. Fictionalized: Your friend accidentally trips in front of her biggest crush.

- Real: You burned dinner in the oven. Fictionalized: You burned Christmas dinner—and this year was the family reunion.

- Real: You got accepted into college. Fictionalized: You got accepted into Harvard after thirteen painstaking interviews.

- Real: You won a local singing competition. Fictionalized: You won American Idol.

The general idea is to take inspiration from something that happened in real life and balloon it up so that it's more interesting. If you are writing about a real conflict, try to think of things that could've made it worse: My sister and I were fighting over the TV remote—what could have made it worse? That's where your creativity comes in.

Get out your journal now and jot down at least five things that could make these scenarios worse:

- You go camping and realize your fire starter is broken.

- You go to dinner and realize you left your wallet at home.

- Your best friend is flirting with your significant other, and you decide to have a confrontation.

- Your alarm doesn't go off, and you're late for school.

- Your GPS leads you to the middle of nowhere, and your phone just died.

- Your classmate just depantsed you.

Sometimes, this technique can trigger more memories, but the beauty of fiction writing is that you can take many liberties to alter facts and include new information that moves the story along, enhances the character dynamics, and increases the overall interest of the story for younger readers.

To spark new ideas, try recalling events from childhood in your journal. This is another good way to prepare for writing any genre of children's literature, as it can be a good beginning to remembering yourself as you were at the age of your intended audience.

Go through some of your old things that you still have from when you were a child. Diaries, notebooks, toys, trinkets, clothing, artwork, and other memorabilia can trigger memories and fresh ideas.

If you are a nonfiction writer, and you are struggling to piece together snippets of memory, start by writing about what you do remember. Then, talk to others who were witnesses to the event in some way, but keep in mind that even if it is a memoir, your story is just that: *your story*, told from your point of view, written in your words. Nonfiction is a bit different. Unless you are writing an autobiography or a biography of someone you know (these are fairly rare in youth literature), your information will almost always come from primary and secondary sources on your subject.

There is plenty of information written about Benjamin Franklin, for example, as well as historical archives that you can reference to help your story along. However, this material does not generally fall under the category of writing from life experience. Apply the techniques suggested in the paragraph above to make the writing relate to your audience.

CASE STUDY: KATIA NOVET SAINT-LOT

www.katianovetsaintlot.com
www.katianovetsaintlot.blogspot.com

Travel has influenced my writing to a large degree. My first book, *Amadi's Snowman*, is set in Nigeria, where I lived for more than three years. If I had not traveled there and been exposed to the reality of so many children like Amadi, I could never have written that story. Travel feeds my writing, because it is an integral part of my life.

It is hard to describe the process of writing, because it is so fickle. Some stories seem to almost write themselves. Others need a very long gestation period. Settings and situations seem to come first for me. Then, characters develop and soon take on a life of their own. Then come the revisions. I am a slow writer, and revising is what I enjoy the most. I love playing with words, sounding them out, and finding the right rhythm and music for a sentence. I am also becoming much better at cutting. More than anything, it is a learning process that never ends. I find that quite humbling.

Most of my stories spring from an experience — something that I see around me or something that my children, who are biracial and global nomads, come to feel or experience. I am particularly concerned and fascinated by all issues relating to third culture kids. These are children, like mine, who grow up in highly mobile families and a truly cross-cultural world. Statistics show they are one of the fastest growing populations in the world, and yet their experience is virtually absent in children's literature. According to Matthew Neigh, executive director of Interaction International, an organization for third culture kids, TCKs represent the single fastest growing population in the world today.

Children's books are important because they are the first books that children will hold, touch, feel, smell, and play with (maybe even chew or break, and that is when we can tell them how important and precious they are, and how they should be treated with special care). Children's books create opportunities for observations and conversations; they widen horizons and take us places, real or imaginary. If children start enjoying children's books at an early age, chances are they will develop a culture of reading quite naturally. As demonstrated in *Amadi's Snowman*, reading opens up the world.

When it comes to promoting my work, a few things come to mind. Thanks to the internet, promoting books all over the world can be done more easily nowadays. I have a website and a blog, and there are benefits to both. The website is more static — not something I update as often. It offers a platform to present my life, my work, and me. The blog is more current, somehow like a journal. I broach issues that interest me, post pictures relevant to something I just saw or experienced, and record my experiences and thoughts as a writer, mother, and expatriate. I have made contacts all over the world, thanks to my blog. It is also a great medium to promote a book.

For instance, I put together a month-long blog tour in November 2008 with the help of my publisher's publicist, to celebrate the release of *Amadi's Snowman*. There were interviews and school visits in places as diverse as the United States, Nigeria, Haiti, India, and Italy. Children and their teachers participated in activities, and I posted the drawings and letters that I received. The kids sent questions to each other, and I facilitated the dialogue between them. I call it "building bridges across the world." Of course, having the books travel physically is more difficult. Books are heavy, and shipping them is costly. In some places, you cannot even count on an efficient postal system, and we had to be quite resourceful for the books to reach the schools in Nigeria or Haiti. I have also visited schools in India, and I am looking into doing virtual school visits through Skype, which is an internet telephone and video software application.

Katia Novet Saint-Lot is a globetrotting author and translator of children's books. Her books for children, such as Amadi's Snowman, have received positive reviews from School Library Journal, Booklist, and Kirkus Reviews, who have praised her attention to intercultural awareness.

Looking to the media

Stories are all around you. Television, magazines, newspapers, and the internet—all are overflowing with information, details, narratives, and general interest content. A child saves his mother's life by calling 911; a young entrepreneur starts a charity and makes a measurable difference; a female scientist makes a groundbreaking discovery.

News items and articles are full of future story potential, even if they are about adults. Think outside the box. What if you substitute the adult in a news article for a child? What if you used the essential plot of a story or article and imagined the rest of it? What would be the children's roles in the events? Be open to other forms of media, such as advertising, music, posters, emails, websites, and movies.

The media can also clue you in to the hot topics of the day. Children are always interested in current trends and events. Or, consider looking for ideas on historical references that hold potential interest, but perhaps are lacking in information—this is a solid technique for

both fiction and nonfiction writers alike. You, as the fiction writer, can create a story based around the possibilities of location, people, places, and events surrounding a historical site or discovery. You, as the nonfiction writer, have plenty of room for investigation and research.

Brainstorming and mind-mapping

Ideas come naturally to some writers. You may know the ones: They have notebooks, folders, and shoeboxes bursting with material. Maybe you're not that kind of writer or you're just in a funk. If you have too many ideas or not enough, it's worthwhile to sit down and brainstorm. The purpose of this is to get rid of the organization and just shoot off as many ideas as you can.

Try starting with a single idea, topic, place, or event, and enjoy the randomness that ensues. You can brainstorm with a friend, a child, or anyone who is willing. The exercise can be fun, and you may choose to write the results in your journal when you are through and have processed your ideas, or jot them down as you go along. If you work best under structure, try setting a timer for 15 minutes, and brainstorm as many ideas as you can during that time. You may not want to stop when the timer is up. Written material can come in the form of word lists, prose, or mind maps.

Mind maps typically originate with a single idea, topic, place, or event, written in a circle in the center of a piece of paper. Around that word, draw other ideas that branch off from it. For example, you may start with the word "toy." This word is written in the center and is the main or starting idea. Lines may be drawn out around the center circle to other words, like "magic," "blue," "space object," and anything else that comes to mind during your brainstorming session. Make as many mind maps as creativity allows, or get even more inventive and create a large-scale mind map on a bigger piece of paper such as newsprint or poster board.

With your mind map, word list, or journal entry complete, look over the results. Are there any ideas or words in particular that spark your interest? Perhaps you see the makings of a story or even a rough plot in the details. Ask yourself the "What if?" question as you go along. What if certain events are substituted for others? What if any elements on the paper were changed? How would it affect the story? Try transcribing your ideas into prose form in your writing journal. This may spark other ideas or possibly develop into a rough draft.

Getting ideas down on paper

Snagging those great ideas might mean keeping a notebook on the nightstand, in your purse or pocket, or wherever you go. If you are the type of person who gets ideas at random (ever had a brain shattering idea come to you in the shower?), make sure you write those ideas down before they disappear as quickly as they arrived.

You may find you already have notebooks stuffed full of ideas that have never had the chance to become stories. Perhaps they will never amount to anything more than a line in a story, or maybe they will not end up as part of anything at all. You will never know until you try them out. Give your ideas a chance, and see what happens with them.

If you are already working on a story, look through any writing journals or notebooks you have to see if anything is usable. Ideas have a way of losing their spark if they sit too long in a notebook or if you take too long to write them down. However, if you have more ideas than you can work on in a reasonable amount of time, losing the spark may be inevitable. One way to counteract this is to be as specific as possible when writing down an idea to ensure you retain most

of its spirit. When you get around to working with it, you will have a clearer picture of where to begin.

When you start to write, write without stopping. Usually, an internal editor will want to take over and re-read each sentence or paragraph as it is being written. Save the editing for last. Try writing for five minutes without stopping to look over what you have written. This is one way to start ideas flowing, and it can be a good way to begin every writing session until you get the hang of it and develop your own routine.

You can try using a different writing prompt each day to begin your writing sessions, such as writing from the point of view of an animal, imagining what it would be like to have only one week left to live, or imagining that you have invented a wonderful new machine that is bound to change the way we live everyday life.

Once you are working on a manuscript, you may find that you no longer need these techniques. You may want to come back to writing prompts every now and then to get the creative juices flowing. Many writers use pre-writing activities on a regular basis. Pre-writing is anything you do to help the writing along, such as character outlines, brainstorming, and note taking. It is often helpful (and recommended) to know your characters, your plot, and your overall story very well before writing a word. Of course, those elements are always open to change in later drafts.

Many hopeful writers see their ideas go nowhere, or result in partially finished stories, because they have too many ideas at once or become unnecessarily stunted by one aspect of the story. Maybe the character is not fitting together quite right, more research is needed, or the ending is becoming a stumper. Make note of where you get stuck, and move on. You can come back to it later, but don't let one trouble

spot bring the entire story to a halt. This is where a writer's group or feedback from someone who knows about writing can come in handy.

Getting into the habit of writing every day is good practice, even if you only take 15 minutes to do it. Don't forget to take "brain breaks." Stretching for a few minutes when you feel yourself starting to lose focus or going to get a glass of water can help you to refocus when you return to your writing.

Common Mistakes to Avoid

Writing for kids is a serious challenge, and many beginners make some these common mistakes.

Preaching to the choir

Okay, so maybe not actually preaching to the choir, but writing a children's book that basically serves as a sermon is never a good idea.

Kids want to be entertained, not taught their daily morality lesson. There's this huge misconception that children's lit needs to teach kids lessons, and that's not the case.

Marie Lamba, young adult author and associate literary agent, explains, "The point is to write an entertaining story that resonates. If, through that story, readers get a gentle reinforcement about something that transcends the page, that's great. The challenge, therefore, is to craft a book that'll be both meaningful *and* widely loved" (2016).

It's not always about teaching—books need to serve first as a form of entertainment. Anything beyond that should be supplementary, not the sole focus.

Rhyme crime
When people rhyme all the time, it's a serious crime.

Writing that was overwhelmingly annoying. Avoid rhyming just for the heck of it. A lot of writers feel like children's books must have rhyming patterns in order to be a children's book, but that isn't the case. The same goes for music—some of the most moving songs out there don't rhyme at all; they simply aim to tell a story in the best way possible. In many cases, this means straying away from the offbeat rhymes.

The only time that rhyming actually works is when it adds something to the story. "It should feel necessary and be pitch perfect, fresh and even unexpected" (Lamba 2016). If you do try writing in rhyme, make sure you read it out loud, have your peers read it over, and keep coming back to it for revisions. If you can tell the story without rhyme, try it. If you notice that the story works better without it, go with your gut.

The overweight draft

When in doubt, cut. Children's books should be short and to the point—every single word in the draft should be adding something to the story. If there's a word sitting there doing nothing, cut it. Most picture books are fewer than 500 words, so it's of paramount importance that your words are doing work.

When in doubt, put your draft on a diet, a cleanse, a fast—just do something. Simplicity will move your readers, and it'll have a much greater impact than overly complex story elements or even overly complex sentences.

Dumbing it down

This right here is the first sentence of a paragraph. A paragraph is a section of writing usually dealing with a single theme or idea, and it's indicated by a new line or paragraph break. A paragraph break is . . .

You get the point. Kids are smarter than you or I probably give them credit for. Don't make the mistake of dumbing down your text. John Rudolph, literary agent for Dystel & Goderich Literary Management, explains, "I've been reading Harry Potter to my son lately, and I'm repeatedly blown away by [J. K.] Rowling's use of big words, virtually all of which can be understood in context without running to the dictionary" (Strawser 2016).

Don't underestimate kids. They're probably one (or two!) steps ahead of where you thought they were.

Not standing out

It's the same old, same old from literary agents across the board—they're all looking for something that stands out. Here are some general tips to make sure that your writing is a hot pink fireball in that dull pile of coal.

1. Make sure your story compels the reader in some way.

2. Unreliable narrators are generally more liked by readers and literary agents.

3. Diversify your stories—whether it be in relation to race, religion, culture, ability, economic status, geography, or anything else that sets your story apart.

4. Push the envelope.

5. Get rid of all the same old tired clichés in both the plot of your story as well as down to the phrases you use in your text.

6. Get rid of the complexity. Less is more, and spare yet strong writing will impress any reader.

A Word About Procrastination

Writing, as mentioned before, takes dedication. If you are like most writers, you are a hopeless procrastinator. Maybe it's that latest Facebook video that has you losing your focus, or maybe it's your fear of missing out—whatever it may be, you have to put writing first if you want to be successful.

You'd be surprised to see how much you can actually get done if you focus for even half an hour.

Some authors love deadlines, because it gives them some structure. If you don't have some kind of contract set up and are writing on your own time, you might think about setting a personal deadline for yourself. This can keep you motivated, and it feels like you're actually working toward a set goal.

If you're writing a chapter book, research how long it should be—this will depend on the publisher, but in general, there are guidelines—and set a word count goal. Here are some general guidelines to keep in mind:

- Picture books should be between 500 to 600 words or enough text to fill 32 pages.

- Lower middle grade books that are simpler in nature and theme should be between 20,000 to 35,000 words.

- Upper middle grade books should be between 40,000 to 55,000 words.

- Young adult books should be between 55,000 to 70,000 words.

Once you decide what your goal word count is, break it up. For example: If you want to write a lower middle grade book, you might set a goal of 30,000 words. You want to finish the writing process (not the editing process) in one month, so you would aim to write about 1,000 words per day. That's about two pages, which is entirely doable, and the word count goal might help to beat your procrastination to the curb.

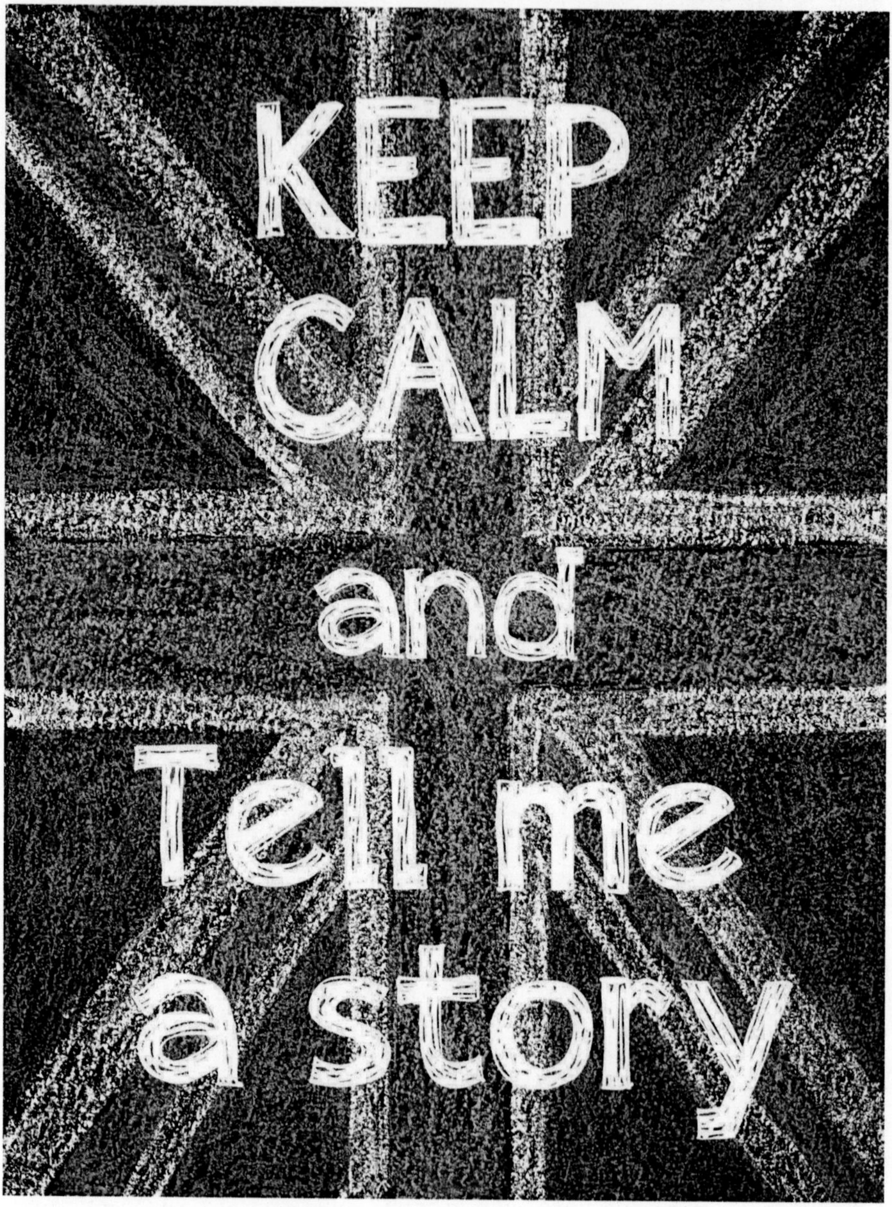
KEEP
CALM
and
Tell me
a story

CHAPTER 5

Creating the Story

Crafting the story might be something that comes naturally to you, but for many, it just isn't. In fact, there has been a debate going on for the past few years on whether or not you can teach this skill. Author and professor Hanif Kureishi explains:

> "A lot of my students just can't tell a story. They can write sentences but they don't know how to make a story go from there all the way through to the end without people dying of boredom in between. It's a difficult thing to do and it's a great skill to have. Can you teach that? I don't think you can" (Jones 2014).

While the skill might not be easily taught, universities and experts everywhere still try—and that's kind of what this next chapter is going to attempt. We're going to give you all the basics here on paper, but in reality, great storytelling isn't easily taught.

The best way to become a better storyteller is through imitation— that means completely immersing yourself in children's literature. I

know this is like the tenth time we've told you to read, but we can't say it enough. If you read this chapter to understand the basic concepts of storytelling, it won't be enough. You need to have that reading experience under your belt to really drive the craft home.

Regardless of these facts, we're still going to try. Expect to see a ton of examples in this chapter in order to bridge the gap between teaching and reading. This is your super-quick guide to creating a story.

So, to get started (and we're going to cover just about everything), let's take a look at beginnings.

Beginnings

The first line of your story can make or break it.

This is particularly true if your entire story is only 500 words — every single word needs to have a meaning, and that meaning needs to be immediately interesting.

The writing blog "Helping Writers Become Authors" gives us five typical ways to screw up the first line (2014). They are:

- The Weather Line: "It was a bright and sunny day."

- The Setting Line: "The grocery store was busy today."

- The Character Line: "Jenna had just turned thirteen."

- The General Statement Line: "Around here, strawberries don't ripen until late spring."

- The Dialogue Line: "Hi, Steve. You got a second?"

Gag.

If you can't interest your readers with your first line, they might put your book back on the bookshelf (if it ever even got there). There are several ways to get people excited with your first line, but your main goal is to do one thing: make the reader curious.

The objective here is to make them think, "Huh?" or something along those lines. You want to force them to read on to the next line, the next paragraph, the next page. If you can get them past that first line, you have a chance to hook them.

This is completely up to you and your story, but it's worthwhile to spend a ton of time on your first line. Come up with many, many options, and keep coming back. Ask people around you what they think—you can even create a Facebook poll. Do what you have to do to ensure that your first line is killer.

To get your blood pumping, here are 10 thought-provoking first lines from 20th century classics:

1. "It was the day my grandmother exploded."
   —Iain M. Banks, *The Crow Road* (1992)

2. "A screaming comes across the sky."
   —Thomas Pynchon, *Gravity's Rainbow* (1973)

3. "Many years later, as he faced the firing squad, Colonel Aureliano Buendía was to remember that distant afternoon when his father took him to discover ice."
   —Gabriel García Márquez,
   One Hundred Years of Solitude (1967)

4. "I am an invisible man."
   —Ralph Ellison, *Invisible Man* (1952)

5. "If you really want to hear about it, the first thing you'll probably want to know is where I was born, and what my lousy childhood was like, and how my parents were occupied and all before they had me, and all that David Copperfield kind of crap, but I don't feel like going into it, if you want to know the truth."
   —J. D. Salinger, *The Catcher in the Rye* (1951)

6. "Stately, plump Buck Mulligan came from the stairhead, bearing a bowl of lather on which a mirror and a razor lay crossed."　　—James Joyce, *Ulysses* (1922)

7. "Every summer Lin Kong returned to Goose Village to divorce his wife, Shuyu."　　—Ha Jin, *Waiting* (1999)

8. "Ships at a distance have every man's wish on board."
   —Zora Neale Hurston,
   Their Eyes Were Watching God (1937)

9. "There was a boy called Eustace Clarence Scrubb, and he almost deserved it."
   —C. S. Lewis, *The Voyage of the Dawn Treader* (1952)

10. "It was a queer, sultry summer, the summer they electrocuted the Rosenbergs, and I didn't know what I was doing in New York."
    —Sylvia Plath, *The Bell Jar* (1963)

Now that you're curious 10 times over, here are 10 great first-liners from children's literature:

1. "Where's Papa going with that ax?"
   —E.B. White, *Charlotte's Web* (1952)

2. "My dad and I live in an airport."
   —Eve Bunting, *Fly Away Home* (1991)

3. "First of all, let me get something straight: this is a journal, not a diary."
   —Jeff Kinney, *Diary of a Wimpy Kid* (2007)

4. "We went to the moon to have fun, but the moon turned out to completely suck."
   —M.T. Anderson, *Feed* (2002)

5. "It certainly seemed like it was going to be another normal evening at Amelia Bedelia's house."
   —Herman Parish, *Amelia Bedelia Unleashed* (2013)

6. "In the light of the moon, a little egg lay on a leaf."
   —Eric Carle, *The Very Hungry Caterpillar* (1969)

7. "In an old house in Paris that was covered with vines lived twelve little girls in two straight lines."
   —Ludwig Bemelmans, *Madeline* (1939)

8. "There is no lake at Camp Green Lake.
   —Louis Sachar, *Holes* (1998)

9. "If you are interested in stories with happy endings, you would be better off reading some other book."
   —Lemony Snicket, *A Series of Unfortunate Events* (1999)

10. "Most motorcars are conglomerations (this is a long word for bundles) of steel and wire and rubber and plastic, and electricity and oil and gasoline and water, and the toffee papers you pushed down the crack in the back seat last Sunday."
    —Ian Fleming, *Chitty-Chitty-Bang-Bang* (1964)

Now that you have some memorable one-liners floating around in your head, have some fun and take a field trip to the library or a

bookstore. Go through aisles of books and read their first lines, making notes of ones that stick out to you. Try to copy down lines that make you curious—lines that make you want to keep reading.

While getting your first line right is important, the bore factor can't suddenly show up for the next few pages. Many writers fall into the trap of providing too much description and setup in the first chapter, a technique that can hurt the flow of your story and possibly cause a reader to put your book down and never pick it up again. Sometimes it's the entire first chapter, but most often, it's about the first 10 pages.

Many successful stories start in the middle of the action. If you find yourself with a book that actually starts at Chapter 2, or if you are writing a picture book that begins a bit slowly, look through your material and honestly assess what is there. Is there any description that could be worked naturally into the dialogue? Can it be trimmed down or the language condensed? How much of the information could be included throughout the story as it progresses? Will there be illustrations that will take care of the description?

Write naturally at first—don't get too caught up with having a perfect first line or a perfect first chapter. It can be much easier to look back at your beginning and see that you wrote your way into the story—then, you can quickly see where things need to be cut so that you can establish your new and improved beginning.

Let's compare two openings (just for fun):

> "James woke up at sunrise and left the farmhouse to milk the cows and lay fresh hay in the barn. After his chores were over, he crossed into the fields with Bailey, his dog, trailing after him."

Now, let's look at a better one:

> "James snapped awake to the sound of a gunshot firing through the crisp morning air. The cows could wait."

Bam. Kill them with your mad word skills, and you should have them hooked.

Voice

Great stories always emerge from a strong voice. If you have an idea of how you want your characters to sound, or if you already have a feel for the narrative in mind, you may be on to something.

Editors can usually smell an inauthentic voice a mile (or a manuscript) away. Is your narrator funny, quirky, serious, single-minded, brazen, fearless, timid, sarcastic, or lovable? There are many possibilities for voice; often, it takes knowing your character inside and out to help him or her find a voice.

Brandon Marie Miller, an award-winning writer of history for middle grade readers, has this to say about voice, specifically when writing nonfiction: "What about finding your own voice if you are a nonfiction writer? Voice is something personal to each writer. It springs from the words we choose, the rhythm of our sentences, and the way we engage the reader and tell our story. As with any writing, you want to use a lively, warm, informative style, even when discussing difficult topics. Some books are chatty and funny, offering short bursts of information. Others have a more serious tone, but that does not mean the writing itself lacks energy."

Once you get the feel for style, tone, and voice, try writing a rough draft or story "sketch"—a loosely written, informally developed piece. Try to focus your ideas at first, and avoid writing plots that are too complicated and include complex subplots or devices like flashbacks. Save this until you are more practiced at writing and have a better handle on your own style.

CASE STUDY: AARON SHEPARD

Award-Winning Author and Online Presence
www.aaronshep.com

"Ten Tips for Young Authors"

1. Turn off the TV.

2. Read a lot, but don't *just* read.

3. Be a spy.

4. Write!

5. Learn to type well.

6. Get a good thesaurus.

7. Simplify.

8. Learn the rules before you break them.

9. Find what interests both you and others.

10. Ask for criticism.

Aaron Shepard is the award-winning author of The Legend of Lightning Larry, The Sea King's Daughter, The Baker's Dozen, and many more children's books from publishers large and small. His stories have also appeared often in Cricket and Australia's School Magazine.

On the web, Aaron maintains an extensive collection of resources for teachers, librarians, storytellers, children's writers, parents, and kids. His site has been viewed by over seven million visitors and has drawn over 25,000 visitors a week. Among its offerings is the web's premier collection of free reader's theater scripts, used in schools and libraries around the world.

Choosing Narration

How do you know when it is better to use first, second, or third-person narration?

It depends on the story. Let's take a look at all three.

First-person narration

Using the first-person voice "I" gives the writing a sense of immediacy. The reader is privy only to the thoughts of the main character telling the story. It is also the voice of the main character relating the story that provides the voice and style of the book.

Some books that use first-person narration are *This is My Family* by Gina and Mercer Mayer and *That Pesky Rat* by Lauren Child. The advantage to using first-person is that the reader can get to know the character well and develop a connection and understanding to him. Keep in mind that first-person narrators can relate only information and details that they see and come in contact with. If your story depicts events that might be more effective if told with a broader focus, consider using third-person. This especially works if lengthy passages require a lot of description.

Second-person narration

Second-person voice, "you," is rarely used in adult literature and is somewhat more commonly found in children's literature. Several examples of books that have second-person narration are *Tell Me Again About the Night I Was Born* by Jamie Lee Curtis, *If You Give a Pig a Pancake* by Laura Numeroff, and *The Wing on a Flea: A Book About Shapes* by Ed Emberley.

In second-person narration, the writing addresses the reader. In the case of Jamie Lee Curtis's book, however, the speaker addresses her parents, probing them to tell her again about the night of her birth and adoption. The book is written in second-person voice, addressing the "you" which is actually her adoptive parents.

Third-person narration

Third-person narration, "he," "she," or "they," is told from the point of view of a narrator who is often invisible as a character, but who can see and relate everything that is happening. Third-person narration allows for variety in the story and can be useful for revealing the thoughts, motives, and feelings of different characters.

Some examples of stories using third person narration are *Stellaluna* by Janell Cannon and *A Pocket for Corduroy* by Don Freeman. Third-person omniscient narration allows the reader access to the thoughts, feelings, senses, motives, and actions of all characters in a story. Omniscient narration renders the reader privy to the conversation going on in the teacher's lounge and can then skip to the conversation on the football field in the next scene or chapter.

Third-person limited reduces the information to the point of view of one character only, and the reader only sees things from his or her perspective.

Third-person multiple point of view allows insight into two or more of the story's primary characters. With third-person multiple, the characters whose viewpoints are revealed usually share the story's narration more or less equally, but each has a differing perspective.

Characterization

How do other authors do it? Characters like Opal from Kate DiCamillo's *Because of Winn-Dixie* or the four friends from *The Sisterhood of the Traveling Pants* by Ann Brashares nearly spring to life, fully formed, right off the page. There is no secret, but successful characters often begin life as sketches or ideas in the author's mind.

Before you begin writing, make a character profile for your main and supporting characters. List as many things as you can think of that are relevant to your character's life, even if you don't think you'll end up using them in the story.

Here are some things you might include:

- Age

- Name

- Hobbies

- Likes and dislikes

- Family background

- Favorite subject in school

- Strengths and weaknesses

- Best friends

- Favorite food

By the time you are finished, you should you know your character as well as you know yourself. To test the theory, ask yourself what each character is really about: What is it that she wants most out of life? What is his major flaw? Does she have enemies? Who does he love?

It may help to keep in mind that children like reading about characters who have something extra or are heroic in some way. In general, while creating your characters, make sure you're steering clear of stereotypes.

There are also a few rules of thumb when it comes to creating supporting characters. Supporting characters can be used as foils — characters who, by their own personalities, highlight or accentuate certain traits in the main character. Supporting characters can also be used to move the story along, reveal plot points, or reveal the setting (especially if the story takes place in the past or future). Consider the duties and role in the story of supporting characters such as Hagrid in the *Harry Potter* series (he is a source of valuable information, and is always saying, "I shouldn't have told you that"), and Jiminy Cricket from *Pinocchio*, who is Pinocchio's conscience.

Try to keep your primary characters to four or less, as too many can be confusing to a young reader. It's a good idea to only create names for the characters with starring roles; other characters are better off remaining in the background. Be sure to assign your main character with the responsibility of enduring and solving the story's primary conflicts. Your readers will be very unhappy if the main character is not the one to be the hero, solve the problems, or be at the center of the resolution.

As always, don't underestimate the power of people-watching. Take notes in your journal:

- Look for qualities that are extraordinary, perplexing, moving, or hilarious.

- Are there any qualities you can play up or exaggerate in your story?

- How can observable qualities be combined within a character for added effect?

- Are there any qualities from yourself or people you know personally that might make colorful contributions to your creations?

After you have a solid idea of who your protagonist is and what she is about, brainstorm about what it is she wants and what it will take for her to get there. What will her role be in the plot? What ups and downs will she experience in her route to trying to achieve her goals?

Character arcs

A character arc is a series of events a character endures throughout the story. A typical character arc might consist of the following:

1. The character is introduced.

2. Something life-altering happens to her.

3. She struggles with the problem or change and tries to deal with it.

4. An obstacle gets in her way.

5. She continues to try to solve her problem and face more challenges.

6. She gets stuck, she is frustrated, and nothing seems to be working.

7. Loose ends begin to tie up.

8. Continued resolution, and she has a chance to falter again, but reveals through her actions that she has learned from these experiences. She does the right thing, makes a good decision, or otherwise shows her newfound knowledge.

9. The story resolves, and the protagonist continues life as a changed person.

This is a very basic outline of a character arc. If you want to try something different or avant-garde, you might think about ditching this pattern, but keep in mind that this is a proven storytelling method that is sure to please your young audience.

Plot and Story Structure

If you're writing a baby book about things with wheels, your story probably won't have much of a plot. If your story is a picture book, the plot will be simple and straightforward, lacking the complexities of, say, a young adult novel about a teen whose parents are going through a divorce. Keep in mind what your target audience likes to read when you're thinking about what you want to write.

Know the plot before you begin writing so that you avoid patching up plot holes in the story as you go along. An unclear plot has a way of getting out of hand as the narrative progresses through the stages of writing. Unless you have a clear sense of direction before you start writing, you can end up with a directionless story, one without a plot, or one that is full of issues.

You might even end up with a "deus ex machina" ending—that is, an ending in which a character who is stuck is "rescued" by some unlikely turn of events or outside force that seems too unlikely. Think: "It was all a dream!" Your story can be solid on other levels— characterization, dialogue, or historical background—but if it does not have a plot, it may never see a press.

While young audiences appreciate outlandish themes and characters who are extraordinary, like Harry Potter, the story's events should flow naturally within the story. Even if you are writing about dragons and fairies, be careful to set up your plot so that the events fit with the characters and the setting.

If you're a beginner, keep the story simple. Write about things, places, and people you are familiar with. Your story will come across as much more convincing than if you're trying to build a believable faraway land when you haven't really practiced your skill at creating a simpler, more familiar storyline. Once you are comfortable with writing, story development, and all the other fine details and nuances involved in writing a children's story for publication, you may decide to branch out and write about a topic that requires some more planning and research.

With a strong sense of your protagonist in mind, you can start creating a plot outline. Start by writing out what the character does in the story, the conflicts he faces, the steps he takes to resolve his problems, and what he learns from his situation. Next, add the subplot. Also, remember that an outline is just a guide — if the story moves you to take it in a different direction, follow your instincts. Plus, if you're writing a shorter work, like a picture book, it might not even be necessary.

As a general rule, the younger your readers are, the more important it is to end on a positive note. In general, readers may not be ready for a strange or negative ending until they are mature enough to handle whatever slice of life you're trying to serve. Young chapter books often end each chapter on a positive point, with plenty of suspense and tension to keep the reader interested and engaged.

Positive or negative, be sure to spice up your story with plenty of action and drama to add interest to your plot points. The dramatic events, action sequences, and plot points are connected by lower points of rest and relief (think of them like R&R for the reader), and this is especially true for longer works, such as novels. When you're doing your homework (reading children's books), pay special attention to the pacing of the events.

Setting and Scene

Where does it all happen? Consider the classic fairy tale, *Sleeping Beauty*—part of the story takes place in a cottage in the woods, and part of it takes place in a castle. The scenery is important to the story, because the fairies take Sleeping Beauty, renamed Briar Rose, to live with them in their hidden forest cottage for safekeeping from the evil fairy's curse. When Briar Rose returns to the castle on her sixteenth birthday with the good fairies that raised her, a shift takes place in the

story. It is a room in the castle that holds the spinning wheel on which the princess is fated to prick her finger. The realization of the curse takes place immediately after the shift in scenery and is the pivotal moment on which the story is based.

Harry Potter is an example of a middle grade or young adult novel (it is a crossover and sometimes packaged as an adult novel as well) with a strong sense of place. After all, what would Harry, his friends, and his professors be without Hogwarts? Hogwarts represents part of their identity and is, in many ways, a sense of power for them in that it is a source of learning and their safe haven. On another level, the school itself contains many secrets and mysteries that are sources of drama and plot points.

Stories with standout settings often lend themselves to standout characters. Similar to the way a subplot can be used to move the main plot along, the setting can be used as a reflection of your character's lives, personalities, and sources of conflict.

Picture books and other illustrated stories may need less detail about the setting within the text, because many background and visual elements are taken care of by the pictures themselves. Description is most effective when you naturally work it into dialogue and action. Be careful not to add a ton of description in the middle of the action.

When deciding what description to include in your story, consider how you can engage the five senses:

- What does a place smell like? Is there smoke in the air? Are there animals around?

- What does it look like? Are there textures? Is there grass? Is it outdoors or in? Is it large or small?

- What are the sounds? Is there music, laughter, noise, or talking?

- Are there taste or touch elements you can include? What does the lemon tart your character is eating taste like? Does your character hate wearing the woolly sweater her grandmother made her for Christmas?

Starting your story off with a bit of description can draw the reader out of his reality and into that of the story. *Sleeping Beauty* begins with a description of the king and queen and their castle on the hill. It then moves into their joy at the birth of their first child and her christening and the events that surround it. Before a word is spoken, the reader has a vivid understanding and, hopefully, a picture in her mind about where things are taking place and the characters within the story.

Effective Dialogue

Have you ever tried writing down an actual conversation? If so, you know there are a lot of throwaway words in verbal communication. People also use nonverbal communication. While the dialogue in your story should feel natural, it should not be boring, like ordinary conversation sometimes is.

When writing dialogue, consider the way people actually speak and communicate, and then think about how you can improve it. Story dialogue should serve a purpose: It should move the story forward, contribute plot points, add description, or reveal a character and her intentions, personality, or appearance. That is a tall order, but it does prove that, when written effectively, dialogue can pack a punch.

Let your story and writing style dictate when to use dialogue. If you are short on dialogue, look for low-interest passages or areas of

description that could be communicated through dialogue. First, consider the following passage:

> **M**elodie wanted to tell her mother that a storm was coming but didn't want to interrupt her. Mrs. Delano was busy finishing a project that she had to hand in the next day. Mel hesitantly approached her seated figure, which was cast in partial light from the murky sunshine coming in through the window facing the beach.

Now think of how the passage might be made more actionable through dialogue:

"Um . . ." Melodie started. Her mother was sitting at the desk by the window in her office, facing the beach.

"What is it, Mel?" her mother asked in a tired voice.

"Just, I don't want to bother you, but . . ."

Mrs. Delano laid her pen down on the desk. "It's okay, sweetie. What is it?" she repeated.

"The news says a storm is coming."

While the first passage is descriptive, the second is more readable and still includes some of the descriptive elements that provide clues to the setting. The dialogue does a better job of moving the plot forward by providing information in the form of setting and narrative detail, while indicating to the reader that something menacing may be lurking on the horizon. It also provides an indication of character traits. We know from the second passage that Melodie is an attentive, responsible girl who is respectful of her mother, and Mrs. Delano is a busy professional. The dialogue is also true to the characters. Children and teenagers use filler words like "um," and their sentences do not flow as smoothly as those of most adults.

Creating effective dialogue can be as simple as listening. You may want to record notes in your observation journal about the way children talk to each other. Visit a place like the mall, where children, teenagers, and adults are most likely to be, and make notes on the conversations you hear. Do children use more contractions than adults, more slang, and incomplete sentences? Also take note, without being too obvious of course, of nonverbal communication used in place of spoken responses and the type of body language used by young people versus that of adults.

While your observations are sure to help your written dialogue read more accurately, remember to flesh it out where necessary, as in the example above. If you write down exactly what your characters say without adding indicators of body language, character traits, plot points, or other elements, your characters may sound a little artificial.

Writing effective, convincing dialogue that flows naturally and serves a purpose for the story takes practice. Look out for some common mistakes authors make when writing dialogue. Try looking at some passages of dialogue you have already written. If you have not written dialogue before, try taking 15 minutes to write as much dialogue as you can before your time is up. Go back and look at what you have written.

- Is there repeated information, either within the passage of dialogue or in the dialogue and surrounding paragraphs?

- Have you used too many attributions? Attributions or tags consist of "he said" and "she said," or phrases like "she asked" and "he replied."

- Are there any passages that are essentially descriptions of dialogue? Cut them and convert them into conversations.

- Look for sentences like, "Melodie asked her mother if she thought they should tape up the windows before the storm hit." Cut it and transition phrases like these into dialogue.

Other common mistakes that are trademarks of weak writing include heavy-handed dialogue or dialogue that comes across as a speech. You do not want to preach to your audience. Instead, let your story show the characters experiencing the natural results or consequences of their actions or learning from the situation at hand.

Be a good editor of your own work. Learning where to trim the fat in your story takes practice and a good eye. Look for areas that are unnecessary, repetitive, or that do not assist the story in any way. Once you have gone through your dialogue, read it aloud. Ask a child to read along with you (you can each read a specific character's dialogue). Listen for areas that don't sound natural and be open — sometimes children contribute unexpected insight.

Show and Tell

If you have been writing for any measurable amount of time, are a member of a writer's group, or have taken a writing class, chances are you have heard the saying, "Show, don't tell."

While the phrase has entered the realm of cliché, it still holds true and may even be the golden rule of writing. Here's basically what it means as a quick refresher: Don't tell the reader what Melodie is learning from her difficult experience. Show her immersed in the situation, dealing with the difficulties that come her way.

That's really all there is to it.

Endings

From the beginning, your readers should be able to identify who the protagonist is and what she is trying to overcome. The story's main action should happen fairly quickly into the narrative. Where endings are concerned, learn to identify when the story is over.

Some writers have a natural sense of closure, while others go on far too long. In general, a story should be over when the tension and story problems are resolved. J. R. R. Tolkien, while an undoubtedly masterful storyteller, continued *The Lord of the Rings* for more than 85 pages after the happily-ever-after resolution. In the last *Rings* book, most readers find the final resolution, rather than the actual ending, more satisfying as a point of closure.

Avoid ending with an expository conclusion that summarizes or moralizes, and resist the urge to tell your readers what they should be taking away from the story. Ask yourself (or a trusted fellow writer) whether the ending feels natural or forced, and whether any of it can be cut.

Other writers can sometimes see things that you as the author cannot, but you must be open to constructive criticism. Other weak endings include those that trail off without any sense of closure or finality, those that don't tie up all the loose ends, and tacked-on, lackluster, or rushed endings.

Pacing is another element that is important to the ending, just as it is throughout the book. Try putting the climax closer to the end of your story. Placing the climax in the penultimate (second–to-last) chapter is an option. In the final chapter, loose ends are tied up, questions are answered that have been nagging the reader for some chapters, and the protagonist may reflect on lessons learned and perhaps even have the chance to prove himself after the major ordeal he has endured.

Try to end on a high note, even if it stands in relative contrast to prior events. While the happy ending may seem cliché, you may not win

any fans from a children's audience by killing off your protagonist at the end of the story.

Another option for the ending is to end with a twist. Surprise endings are a way to end on a high note, and kids usually love them.

CHAPTER 6

The Final Writing Stages

You want your manuscript to be 100 percent before sending it out to publishers, which means that you need to snuggle up nice and cozy to the revision process. The purpose of revising is to allow yourself to look at what you've written with fresh eyes. Take a few days to separate yourself from your book and then go back in to look for necessary changes. This chapter will give you some pointers on how to master the final writing stages of revision.

Revising and Rewriting

Even after you finish writing your story, the chance that it's actually done are pretty slim. Professional writers often go through tons of drafts, versions, and reams of paper before calling a draft a final manuscript.

Have another writer, or at least a well-versed reader, look over your story and offer pointers. You'll find that stepping back from your story for a while can give you a fresh perspective. While you are "away" from the draft, read, watch movies, and spend time around children if you can. Hopefully, some or all of these activities will provide a fresh outlook and maybe even inspiration that will make your story stand out more than it already does.

When you're finally ready to come back to the beast (by beast, we mean your draft), you'll want to keep an eye for certain things and make some changes:

- Trim the fat (unnecessary words, sentences, phrases, or paragraphs)

- Look for areas that are slow or make you want to skip ahead—cut them or work them into the text in a different way

- Check for plot holes

- Remove dialogue that is strained, repetitive, or unnecessary

- Cut any confusing scenes

- Look for and get rid of points in the story that lead the reader's focus away from the protagonist's goal

- Look for areas unnecessary for the story development— if they don't move the story forward or add some kind of necessary meaning, cut them.

- Scan your entire story for weak or unoriginal verbs and

replace them with more unusual or vibrant ones (walked — paced; pushed — slammed; watched — gazed)

- While we're talking about verbs, scan your story for "to be" verbs and try to replace them with stronger, clearer verbs ("The water is good" — "The water tastes good")

- Look for indefinite language and passive voice in your writing ("A loud crash of thunder could be heard" — "Mel heard a loud crash of thunder")

- Make sure your descriptions are clear and specific, not general statements ("The candy tasted terrible" — "The candy was bitter and stale")

These are elements you can improve once you get that first draft down. If you focus on these revision elements while you're actually writing, you may never finish your first draft. The most important part of writing is just get something on the page — then you have something to work with.

Testing Your Ideas

Who better to try out your ideas on than the people who will be reading your book? The "gatekeepers" — parents, teachers, children's librarians, and, of course, children — are some of your best sources for feedback. If you're working on a picture book, try reading to children aged two through seven to gauge a reaction.

When you have children look at your work, ask these questions:

- Did you enjoy reading this book?

- Was there anything in the book that you didn't like?

- What interested you the most about this book?

- What was your favorite part?

- Did you like the ending?

- If you could change anything about the book, what would it be?

- What kinds of books are your favorites?

Then, ask the same of parents and teachers. Talk to children's librarians—they are often ahead of the curve when it comes to knowing the next big trend for kids. If you are short on children to read to, ask if you can schedule a reading at the library well in advance. Your library or children's librarian may help you promote and advertise the reading.

This will probably never happen to you (wink), but if it turns out that your book isn't loved by the little ones, you might be forced to go

back to your manuscript and start problem-solving. Use their feedback to improve your existing manuscript.

Here are some key things to revisit if you're revising for a second time:

- Are there weak areas that can be strengthened?

- Do you use active language?

- Does the dialogue seem convincing?

- Is the style and point of view consistent?

- Where can you add more drama or action?

- Are the characters developed enough or do they seem like cardboard cut-outs?

- Are there lulls or dull points in the story? How can these be made more interesting?

- Is the climax climactic enough?

Sometimes, an editor will ask for a revision. If you are not under contract, first consider whether the revisions will be worth your while. On one hand, the changes may not result in a contract or publication, but on the other, they may well be a chance to get free, professional feedback and can go a long way toward making your story better.

Dealing with rejection

Don't take rejection personally. It's not you that's being rejected—it's your manuscript. Even the best writers are rejected constantly. This is a feeling that you will have to become familiar with. It's pretty much inevitable.

One of the most important things you can do to avoid rejection is to make sure you're carefully targeting which publishers you submit to. If you're submitting a book about trains, and the publishing company has already published a ton of books about trains, you might be rejected because the publisher is shifting their focus.

Whether you're rejected for business reasons or not, it's always important to stay honest with yourself. Is your writing good enough? How does it compare to similar books from major publishers?

Some primary reasons for rejection are:

- The manuscript needs too much editing.

- The manuscript or publication package is sloppy or poorly written.

- The story is not marketable.

- The plot is too familiar or not original enough.

- The story needs more excitement.

- It's not the right genre or theme for the publisher.

- The vocabulary or approach is not age-appropriate.

- It's not what the publisher is looking for at the time.

It can be helpful to remember that very successful authors, such as Dr. Seuss, had their first manuscripts rejected dozens of times before being accepted by the right publisher.

Publishing is not a field for the faint of heart or the thin-skinned. Writing takes time — time to craft, revise, and perfect the manuscript, time to research publishers, and time to prepare query letters and submission packages.

Targeting possible problems with your writing
If your story is receiving form rejection after form rejection with no hope of publication, try to figure out why.

Here are some starting points:

- Have you received any personalized rejection letters? If so, look to them for clues.

- After discussing your manuscript with a trusted writer or critique group, do they have any advice to offer?

- Is your book's subject or theme not popular anymore? Is the market full of books like yours?

- Have you revised your manuscript, or are you sending out your first draft and expecting it to attract attention? Most writers revise a dozen or more times before sending their work out to publishers.

- Is your query letter or submission package appropriately prepared? Does the cover letter provide an accurate representation of the material contained in your manuscript? If your submission package isn't that great, you may be getting the boot before anyone even sees your story.

Finding a publisher can be like choosing a party dress or a suit; you probably wouldn't walk into a store and grab the first thing you see without checking the size or price and trying it in. It's the same thing with publishers. It's really important that you read some of their already published material so that you know what they're looking for. Otherwise, you're just wasting your time and will be faced with another rejection.

Other challenges

Your single biggest challenge as a writer is *time*. Without time, you'll never make it past chapter one. Without time, you'll never perfect that first draft. Without time, you'll never see your name on a published book. If writing is a priority to you, you have to make time to do it, and it has be a regular part of your schedule.

Your second biggest challenge as a writer is *environment*. Some writers like to sit at a desk with a warm cup of coffee. Other writers like to lie in bed with a laptop, feet propped up on pillows. Even still, some writers like to go somewhere other than home—a library, a coffee shop, or a dedicated office—to get away from the distractions that being at home can bring.

Try different environments and arrangements to see how and where you are your most productive. It can be worthwhile to experiment with different setups. Leave your phone in your purse to see if you can focus longer. Try listening to different types of music—soothing music, such as light jazz or classical piano, can amp up your creativity. Try snacking while you're working to boost your brain energy.

Then, as you return to that place time and again, a habit of writing will form, and you may find yourself growing more productive as you enter that particular environment and setup. For example, you sit down at your desk in the corner, a green smoothie on the coaster next to your desktop, and you put headphones on, signaling to your mind that now is the time to focus and do nothing but write.

For some reason, I have always liked writing from a child's point of view, even when I wrote fiction for adults when I was younger. After I had kids and was reading all these wonderful children's books to them, it just made sense to try writing for children. I quickly discovered it is quite challenging—and very fun. What other job would involve dreaming up an iguana who plays the blues? I think there is no better calling than writing for children. Although I do not like preachy books, I do hope to inspire kids and make them think as well as entertain them.

My advice to aspiring children's book authors:

- Make time to write on a regular basis

- Go to a restaurant or a park if you get distracted at home

- Read many children's books

- Hang out with kids, so you can see the world through their eyes

- Find some writing buddies for critiques or just support

My book, *Cesar Takes a Break,* was inspired by a real incident in my son David's fourth-grade classroom. His teacher had a pet iguana, named Cesar, and he escaped from his cage on the last day of spring break. When the kids returned to school on Monday, he was gone. He was missing for five days before he returned to the classroom through a vent in the wall. David is the one who spotted him, and he was a hero for the day. After Cesar was safe, I thought the story was funny. It looked to me as though Cesar had taken a spring break. That got me thinking about how class pets feel about vacations and what they do when the kids are gone.

From the beginning, I wanted Cesar to tell his own story in a journal. My kids wrote in journals in kindergarten through second grade, and I think that is a great experience. And I wanted Cesar to explore the school on his break, because I am impressed by the cool things schools offer—such as the music rooms, gym, playground, cafeteria, and the stage.

Although there are big differences between writing fiction and journalism, I think my experience as a journalist helps in two ways—with research and revisions. To get the details you need to make a fictional story seem real, you usually need to go beyond reference books.

You have to find real people and be prepared to ask some pretty strange questions. As a reporter, you learn there is no such thing as a stupid question. When my editor wanted me to incorporate more realistic iguana behaviors into Cesar's story, I talked to iguana owners and pet store workers, asking them what their iguanas did when they were happy, how they could tell when they were mad, and what their favorite foods were. The interviews were a lot of fun, and they gave me details I could not find online or in books.

I also think that years of writing and editing newspaper stories makes it a bit easier for me to tackle revisions. When you write for a newspaper, you get used to someone questioning your story, asking you to get more details, or rewriting your lead. It is a collaborative process. You learn not to take changes personally (at least most of the time).

So, even though I would love to hear my editor say my first version of a story is perfect, I am not too dismayed when I get a request for revision. Revising is just part of the process. Fortunately, the suggestions and concerns my editor, Meredith Mundy, raised in the early versions of *Cesar Takes a Break* really made sense to me. I was glad once the revisions were made, because I think the result was a better story.

I love the illustrations Rogé created for *Cesar Takes a Break*. I love the colors, the humor, and the warmth. Although I have never met Rogé and only chatted with him by email after the book came out, I did get to have some input into the illustrations. I saw early sketches and was able to make comments and suggestions. I was glad to have that opportunity, but I did not try to dictate how the illustrations would look. I know the artist has to have the freedom to make the story his own. And Rogé did exactly that. His illustrations are much better than anything I could have imagined.

Being an author has been great fun. I love visiting schools and reading my book and talking about writing. I get a kick out of the kids. They come up to tell me stories or show me something they have written or just to give me a hug. Their openness and enthusiasm are inspiring.

Susan Collins Thoms is the author of Cesar Takes a Break, illustrated by Rogé, and The Twelve Days of Christmas in Michigan. She also is the author of two board books, "Noah's Ark" and Jonah and the Big Fish." As a journalist, she has worked as a reporter and copy editor. She now writes health news features for SpectrumHealthBeat.org.

CHAPTER 7
Understanding Illustration

Being a writer and an artist is pretty cool, but if illustrating isn't really your specialty, you're better off leaving that part of the process for someone else.

Illustrators have to be knowledgeable about multiple areas of their profession. For instance, the typical duties of an illustrator include familiarity with various artistic media, drawing, creating storyboards and layouts, creating dummy books, the ability to create a visual narrative, and polishing and fine-tuning art. The goal is to make the book look awesome in front of the camera and on the shelf.

If you think you have the ability to illustrate your own work, you need to put some time into improving. Take a drawing or painting class at your local community college or arts center. Give yourself a chance—spend quality, focused time illustrating your ideas and get a second opinion to figure out where you can improve. Read plenty of books about illustrating for children, and if you can, contact an illustrator. He might have some insight to offer. You might be able to

get some help from a children's literature professor, too. It's worth sending an email to ask.

Traditionally, artists learning visual art have copied the masters to learn their techniques. The same concept applies to illustrating. Look at picture books past and present, and try your hand at copying the drawings to get a true assessment of the variety of techniques and styles. During the course of your investigation, you may want to look at books by other author-illustrators, such as the following:

- *Where the Wild Things Are* by Maurice Sendak

- *The Night I Followed the Dog* by Nina Laden

- The *Clarice Bean* books by Lauren Child

- *The Very Quiet Cricket* by Eric Carle

- The *Zelda and Ivy* books by Laura McGee Kvasnosky

- *Grandfather Twilight* by Barbara Berger

- *Officer Buckle and Gloria* by Peggy Rathmann

To really get a feel for the division of labor that takes place between the text and illustrations, find a picture book by an author-illustrator and one by a separate author and illustrator. Compare just the text in both.

Is the text leaner in the book by the author-illustrator? How does the narrative in the other book compare? Now, examine the pictures. How important are the pictures when it comes to understanding the story? (Side note: this could turn into a nice extra credit project for your literature class.)

Sketchbooks

Look at your sketchbook as a tool. It is a method for recording visual information and ideas. Find one that suits you and is small enough to be portable. Take it with you and record observations in different areas where children will be, like the mall or the park. If you have nieces or nephews or can observe kids somehow (without being creepy), try to capture their movement, personalities, and expressions as much as possible.

If your medium is charcoal, pastels, pens, or pencils, bring them with you in a small zipper case, along with other accessories like a kneaded rubber eraser and a facial tissue for smudging. If you work in water-colors and want to capture color nuances "*en plein air,*" or outdoors, try using a water pen and stamp inks, like the ones available on portable ink pads for scrapbook enthusiasts (Distress Ink is a popular brand).

As part of your work routine, try to make at least one sketch or illustration in your sketchbook per day. Sketch anything: What you see immediately before you, a pet, your backyard, relatives, a garden, or a street scene. This is a good way to get practice on a daily basis so that you are actively working to improve your craft.

Character Development

When developing the characters for your children's book, character sketches and outlines are helpful. Character profiles help you organize your thoughts, think about the traits that make your character unique, and provide catalysts for plot points. Getting new ideas for characters can be kind of hard sometimes. For initial idea-generation, prototypes can include family, friends, co-workers, and acquaintances.

For author-illustrators, the scope of dynamics is increased for their characters. If you have already written a book and are coming to the illustrations secondarily, you have traits already in place, and most likely a picture of the characters in your mind.

When drawing the characters, remember these kinds of things:

- Place them in a variety of different circumstances, with views of the profile, head-on, side views, and everything in between.

- Illustrate them performing a series of actions. This will help you to have a solid grasp of the character at all angles so he appears consistently throughout all documents.

- Characters should have visual appeal, because they will, after all, be selling books. Visual appeal does not necessarily mean attractiveness, but rather a compelling aspect that engages the attention.

- Draw your characters with different expressions—if they are animals, use that to your advantage. If you character is a puffer fish, for instance, she might blow up when upset or excited; an elephant might involuntarily blow water when experiencing the same emotions.

- The eyes are an important part of your illustrations. Changing their expressions, along with eyebrows, conveys widely differing nuances.

Movement and Expressions

It's really hard to express movement and expressions when you're working with a two-dimensional piece of paper. The drawings you illustrate will often match up pretty closely with the actual words of the book. If the narrative describes Mr. Frog slipping down the edge of a steep, muddy hill, part of the image has already been created in the reader's mind. The text and illustrations should complement one another. Providing an illusion of motion creates movement in illustration.

This can be done in several obvious ways, like using motion lines, sketching flailing limbs, or a character in motion, such as Mr. Frog frozen in a two-dimensional stance, tumbling heels over head partway down the muddy slope, with his hat poised in midair and tie sideways. The lines you use also affect the sense of motion. Thin, thick, wavy, or wispy lines are examples of ways you can create movement. Hair streaming out behind a horse also moves the eye around.

Subtle changes can go a long way when depicting expression and personality in characters. Changing just one feature, such as the expression of the eyes, can convey a multitude of emotional nuances, as can a corresponding shift in the eyebrows. Gestures, body language, actions, and reactions are important. As part of an illustrative study, try creating a sketch of your main character in a variety of moods. Publishers will be looking for a dynamic character that provides a visual representation of the action in the text, but also that adds another dimension to the narrative.

Use of Color

Sometimes, the print version of a book can look totally different than the digital one. Digital, or software-created, art should be saved at a high resolution, such as 300 dpi (dots per inch) so that it's ready for print. Ink reproduces better than paint—because ink is absorbed into paper and paint lies flat in a film on top of the surface, the way in which the two media reflect light is different and affects the print outcome. It's the difference between a scanned image of a light-saturated image and a light-reflective image. Use caution when illustrating with permanent markers—the ink fades fast and should be kept out of sunlight and bright light. However, when marker illustrations are fresh, they reproduce accurately in print.

As an illustrator, you should have an understanding of color theory. Colors can be harmonious or complementary, muted or vibrant, cool or warm, and primary or secondary. Understand color-mixing techniques to achieve greater control over the depth of your illustrations. Reference books like *The Complete Color Harmony: Expert Color Information for Professional Color Results* by Bride M. Whelan and Tina Sutton, the *Designer's Guide to Color* by I. Shibukawa and Y. Takahashi, and the *Watercolor Mixing Directory* by Moira Clinch and David Webb.

Color can have a powerful visual impact on the viewer. It provides the backdrop and mood to your narrative. Visual effects impact the reader's perception of your story, and in a final published work, story and image function together as a single entity. Color psychology basically means that color enhances a story's atmosphere and tone. Each color means something different. For example, blue can convey a sense of peace, while golden colors convey a sense of warmth. Because children's books often dwell in the realm of the imagination, colors can be unexpected—think pink elephants and blue dogs.

The way you use color is important. Patches of color in your illustration move the eye around, while a solid color makes line work in the drawing stand out. Limiting the color palette can be used for subtle story effects. For example, if you're illustrating a flashback or dream sequence, using one color with line work or two colors can mark that section as being apart from other illustrations in the book. Decide whether your palette should be monochrome, a single color, whether it should have the appearance of texture, or appear flat. Pay attention to how background colors affect colors in the foreground. Changing the tone of the background can affect how the foreground colors stand out.

Use of Media

When determining what media to use to illustrate your story, you have think about the story itself. What kind of illustration would bring the characters and narrative to life? What would be suitable for the story?

Snowflake Bentley, a Caldecott award-winning picture book illustrated by Mary Azarian, is a story that takes place in Vermont; her illustrations, appropriately, are woodcuts. Other author-illustrators use mixed media or cut paper collages to illustrate their stories. Graphics-oriented software programs are right at your fingertips these days, so more children's books are being designed this way.

Ed Emberley's picture book, *The Wing on a Flea,* was first released in 1961 and reissued in 2001 with vibrant new illustrations, all of which he created with a computer illustration program. Audrey Wood's *Red Racer* was also produced with digital illustrations. Another method of selecting your media is to assess the sketches you've done.

What kind of line quality do they have? If you use an interesting or unusual line quality, try working in a medium that allows you to focus on line and present color as secondary or transparent, such as watercolor or dye with pen and ink. If you have a tendency to use bold, strong colors, consider digital media, cut-paper or mixed media, or thick, heavy media with strong opacity, such as gouache, acrylic, and pastels. If you have an eye for design and the creative arrangement of elements, try collage, digital media, or photo-manipulation.

When to Write and When to Illustrate

When you are handling both text and illustrations, how do you know which one will work the best where? Visual elements, like the setting and physical appearances of characters, are most appropriately handled with pictures. Authors who don't illustrate tend to visualize the story in "scenes" while they're writing. Inevitably, some visual material may come through into the text. One benefit of being the illustrator of your own work is that you can cut those visually descriptive scenes from the text and turn them into the pictures you saw in your mind's eye. Authors who only write can't really do that. They have to cut material from their manuscript and give total control to the illustrator, whom they might never even meet.

The non-visual details—any sensory elements that are left over—are included in the text. The text anchors the illustrative work in many ways, informing background (like city or country) and setting (school or Aunt Maybelle's house). The pictures convey emotions and mood on a visual level that is implied in the text. For instance, a sentence that reads, "The heavy sky threatened rain" might contribute the implications of heaviness and rain to the drawings. If the text conveys a great deal of detail, for instance, in a passage high in action, you will select the most interesting, crucial, pivotal, or exciting point in the action to illustrate.

CHAPTER 8
Marketing to Publishers

W hile the writing process might be your favorite part, you still have to get down to the nitty-gritty and dip your toes in the marketing world.

Directory Listings

You can list your book in a number of different directories. Like obtaining an ISBN and bar code and registering your copyright, a listing is another way to make your work legit, and self-published works need all the help they can get when it comes to legitimacy. Find out how to have your title included in listings that apply to both the children's book industry and the general market, if it includes listings for children's literature. See the back of the book for a guide to directory listings.

Book Reviews and Publicity

Some sources, such as *Kirkus Reviews*, offer reviews for self-published and independent authors. A review through *Kirkus Discoveries* costs $400 per review with a seven to nine week turnaround, or $550 for an expedited review, which is returned in three to four weeks. *Kirkus* holds *Discoveries* reviews to the same standards as they do regular reviews, according to their website at **www.kirkusreviews.com**.

You can use reviews to promote your book—it gives your work some oomph. It's really easy to post reviews you get onto Amazon, Powell's Books, or the Barnes & Noble websites, and you can even use quotes from a review on the back cover of your book.

If yours is a nonfiction picture book with a historical subject, send review queries to publications that review children's nonfiction as well as those that look at historical books, such as historical societies and organizations. Make sure you ask the organization if they're interested before just sending out copies of your book—that way, you're being smart about your initial investment. See the back of the book for a list of publications that review children's books as well as a sample review query.

Be aware of the different types of reviews:

- *Pre-publication reviews* are written for those in the book industry, such as wholesalers, bookstores, and libraries. These reviewers expect to receive bound galleys. A galley is a prepublication book copy that is usually printed in black and white.

- *Early reviews* are packaged with a review slip, press release, copies of other reviews, and other materials, like brochures, that add credibility to your book. See the back of the book for a sample review slip and press release.

- *Post-publication reviews* are intended for the consumer and appear after the book is published.

For major review outlets like *Publishers Weekly*, which reviews children's books and has a web-exclusive Children's Book Review on their website, send a press release with a cover letter and a bound galley four to five months before publication. Visit the children's book exclusive at **www.publishersweekly.com** and click the "Reviews" tab, then click "Children's." Follow up one to two months later by sending them a final copy of the book. It's really important to send the galley first since *Publishers Weekly* is a pre-publication reviewer. Your book may not be reviewed, but if it is, it can mean a major increase in sales to the *PW* market.

Another thing you can try is reaching out to popular bloggers to offer them a free copy of your book in exchange for a review. Spend some time surfing the web, and see what you can come up with. Here's a good place to start to at least browse some of your options: **www.midwestbookreview.com/links/othr_rev.htm**.

You might also think about investing in a rubber stamp to mark your review copies. While the review stamp may not prevent the book from being sold, it will ensure that it is not returned to you for credit. People also might turn around and sell your book on popular online platforms like eBay or Amazon—you don't need any additional competition, especially if that competition is your own book!

Finally, when you receive a positive review, say thank you. Follow up with a handwritten note or email to the people who took the time to review your book, and let them know you appreciate it.

What is the difference between a critic and a reviewer?

* A book critic reads the whole book and provides educated and in-depth commentary.

* Some book reviewers may not read the entire book and will often write their reviews based on the press release, front and back matter (what appears on the front and back of the book), and what they got from skimming the book.

Press Promotion and News Releases

Once you receive a positive review, you can use an excerpt for promotional purposes. Include a quote on the back cover, in press releases, and in other promotional material.

For a sample press release, see the back of the book. Consider going to your local media for articles or reviews. As a local who has published a book, you are newsworthy and interesting. Local newspapers, radio shows, and television stations may be interested in an interview

or article, which can mean a step toward the local promotion of your book.

If you decide to self-publish, you will have to take these extra steps toward promoting your work—steps that a traditional publisher would normally handle. This means finding reviewers, arranging your own interviews, and putting together your press releases and other marketing copy.

Your Website or Blog

A primary method of advertising you should look to before considering spending money on something like magazine advertising is your website or blog.

A website should be central to your public identity as an author, and it should be the go-to resource for all of the following things:

- Your publications
- Professional memberships

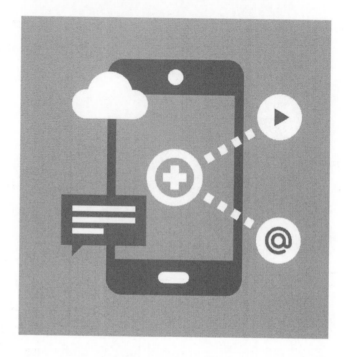

- Availability for speaking

- Presentations

- Book signings

- Press releases

- Bibliography

- Contact information

- Reviews and blurbs

- Any other promotional materials concerning your publications and professional life

You don't actually have to have a website—you can just start out with a blog, which is what most authors do. To learn more on starting and maintaining a successful and profitable blog, check out "So You Want to Start a Blog: A Step-by-Step Guide to Starting a Fun & Profitable Blog" by Rebekah Sack.

Researching Publishers

In your research, gather as many resources as you can on as many publishers as possible and look into their various imprints and divisions.

Start with the library. If you wrote a picture book, check out comparable picture books — those most similar to yours. Which books have the most in common with yours? Who published them — what house or imprint? Your next step will be to order the catalogs from those publishers or imprints. Look through it to see what else they are publishing, and go back to the library to look at their other selections more in-depth. Read as many titles as you can.

Look in publisher catalogs and check their websites for other details, such as:

- How many new authors are they publishing?

- Do any trends consistently stand out?

- Are any particular genres published over and over again?

- Do they publish mostly nonfiction or fiction?

- Are they pushing boundaries or are they more traditional?

- Are most of the books targeted for a specific age group?

To find more publishers and their contact information, invest in a copy of the annual publication *Children's Writer's and Illustrator's*

Market. The CWIM indexes publishers in a variety of ways. For example, the book includes a subject index and age-level index, and you can find publications based on whether they publish poetry, photography, whether they are international, or by awards and competitions.

If your book is a nonfiction picture book or young adult novel, you would first check the subject index. After recording entries that apply to your book, check the age-level index and cross-reference for publishers that appear on your subject list. Highlight these publishers and then investigate them further by looking through their catalogs and reading the books they publish. Some publishers make their catalogs available on their websites.

Another resource to check is the Society of Children's Book Writers and Illustrators, found at **www.scbwi.org**, where a children's book publisher market survey is listed. Another helpful website is the Children's Book Council, found at **www.cbcbooks.org**, which provides information on publishers who are members of that organization.

Targeting Publishers

You're going to be flooded with rejection letters, no matter what you do. If, by some insane act of God, you receive a rejection letter that actually comments on your work, you need to save it, frame it, post it to your mirror, put it under your pillow at night—you need to read that thing 100 times and really take it in. Editors are some of the busiest people you may ever interact with, so if one of them takes the time to write a letter commenting specifically on your work, know that they had a reason for doing so.

Personalized rejections often provide clues as to what is not quite right with your manuscript—it could be anything from style to structure to theme. It is not an editor's job to provide feedback on the many untold numbers of manuscripts that pass through their hands, and this is yet another reason a personalized rejection letter can be so valuable.

Besides investigating websites and catalogs and reading as much of a publisher's material as you can find, try putting Amazon to work for you. Use the Advanced Search option to create lists of publishers according to the criteria you put in. For example, if you want to see everything that Random House's Yearling imprint has published in the past year, invoke the Advanced Search tab by selecting "Books" from the drop down menu next to the search bar on the homepage. In the search bar, type "Yearling Books," and click "Go."

This brings you to a page with a listing of Yearling imprint publications, but notice the additional search options that now appear under the search bar at the top of the page. One of the additional options is "Advanced Search." Clicking this takes you to a multi-field form. The "Books Search" form allows you to specify search options such as keywords, title, author, publisher, and more.

Type "Yearling" in the Publisher field. In the "Pub. Date" field, specify whatever date suits the time frame you want to investigate. Choose "After" and set a date to see everything Yearling has published since that date. Narrow your search further by setting the "Reader Age" field. For example, a search for Yearling publications for the past year, with the language set to "English" and the Reader Age set to "9-12 Years" yields hundreds of results. Investigate the various Advanced Search options and vary them as necessary to compare results.

Look through the results and read the book reviews that accompany each selection to quickly get an understanding of the book. Is it funny, written in rhyme, or educational? Use the process of elimination to see what kind and how many books a publisher is accepting from first-time authors.

Once you have narrowed down that list, narrow it further by coming up with words that describe your book. Is it funny? Does it involve music? Try to find books that deal with topics and themes similar to yours, and pay close attention to the houses that are publishing them. Doing this can give you a good idea of a house's personality and character.

What publishers avoid rhyme? Which ones favor anthropomorphic characters? Do the ones that publish stories about talking bears deal with humorous topics, or do they use the characters to lighten otherwise heavy material? Which ones combine humor with educational topics? When you are finished, you will have a better understanding of what type of work the publisher accepts from first-time authors.

CASE STUDY: LISA SCHROEDER

Children's Author
www.lisaschroederbooks.com

There is so much information available online now, it is going to serve you well to find websites and blogs where you can learn about agents and who might be a good fit for your work.

Due to the lower income that picture book authors receive, many agents are not interested in picture book writers, which I know can be discouraging. But fear not—if you are writing something new, fresh, and fun, and your work is fabulous, it is not impossible. I have a couple of friends who are primarily picture book writers, and they have agents, so I know it can be done. If at all possible, visit a conference where agents specializing in books for children are attending.

At the time I sold my first book, in 2004—a picture book called "Baby Can't Sleep"—many publishers still accepted unsolicited manuscripts. I had been submitting various picture book manuscripts for a few years with no luck, although I received personal rejection letters from time to time, which kept me going. One of the manuscripts came back from a publisher with a personalized rejection letter that gave me some very encouraging words. I hung on to that letter, and through talking with other writers online, learned what kinds of books the publisher seemed to be buying at that time. I had a manuscript that seemed to be a good match, so I submitted it, and a few months later, I received a phone call from an editor telling me that the company wanted to publish my book.

Usually, a book starts with a few seeds of ideas, and grows from there. I keep a notebook where I jot down words, phrases, titles of songs I like, or stories I see in the news. For example, my novel "Far from You" came about from 1) wanting to write a book with elements from the classic story "Alice in Wonderland," 2) wanting to write a book where the main character is a singer/songwriter, and 3) thinking about a news story where a family was stranded in a blizzard for days. Ideas are everywhere; we just have to be open to them.

Sometimes writing means addressing difficult topics. As far as writing about death, as writers, our job is to do our best to tap into the feelings of our characters and put that on the page the best way we can. I believe death is as much a part of life as breathing, eating, and sleeping. We will all experience the death of a loved one at some point in our lives, probably multiple times. We may not be 16 when it happens, but it will happen. I suppose I want teens to see that yes, it is hard and it hurts, but you will get through it. And I really believe those who pass on before us want us to continue to live our lives and to be happy, so you will see that as a recurring theme in my books.

Letters from readers tell me my books have helped them to see and appreciate the loved ones in their life in a new way. Those who have lost a loved one often tell me the books have helped them feel a little less alone. Ultimately, I want to tell a good story — one that a person thinks about after she turns the last page and sets the book down. That is what I think about as I write. If I think too hard about what I want a reader to come away with, I risk turning the book into some kind of lesson, and I never want to do that.

There really is not anything about writing that is easy for me. Plus, each book has its own set of unique challenges. For YA, you have to have a great voice combined with a unique, engrossing story. I have heard it said we are in the golden age of YA right now, and while it is a good place to be, it is also a very competitive place to be, and getting more so by the day. With each book, I have to strive to do better, and that is never going to be easy.

As far as younger readers are concerned, a lot of people seem to think writing a picture book is easy. Coming up with a unique story idea with fun characters and a plot that can be told in 500-700 words is incredibly challenging. And a picture book should have a plot if it is going to have any chance in today's marketplace.

Lisa Schroeder is an author who writes for kids of all ages. Her picture book titles, published by Sterling, are Baby Can't Sleep and Little Chimp's Big Day. Her middle-grade novel, published by Aladdin, is called It's Raining Cupcakes. And her young adult novels, published by Simon Pulse, are I Heart You, You Haunt Me; Far from You; and Chasing Brooklyn. You can read more about Lisa and her books at her website — ***www.lisaschroederbooks.com.***

CHAPTER 9
Self-Publishing

W e've referenced this a couple of times up to this point, so drumroll please . . . your introduction to self-publishing is finally here! If you self-publish, you're going to be doing everything that a traditional publisher does for you, from manuscript development, to editing or finding an editor, to art and cover design, to binding, distribution, marketing, and promotion.

Self-published books typically reach a limited readership, but thanks to software programs, they can be produced affordably and professionally. Advances in technology have brought somewhat increased levels of respect to some self-published books because the quality can be (emphasis on *can be*) much better now than it used to.

What Does Your Book Need?

You probably won't get rich publishing your first children's book. Authors don't go into publishing to make money. Most people who write and publish do it for the love of the craft. While there are exceptions, and success does happen, it takes a tremendous amount of hard work and time. It can take years to get a book accepted for publication, and once it is, the advance you receive has to sustain you for a year or more. Only once the book sells enough copies to pay for your advance do you start making royalties.

It's true that you get to keep a larger percentage of royalties with self-publishing than you would with traditional publishing, but remember that your audience is also much more limited, which means you might not end up making as much money. Realistically, there are other things to consider about self-publishing.

While the quality of self-published work has increased due to advancing technology—lacking an editorial process, the contributions of a design team, a national or international distribution market, and the recognition of industry professionals—it's not always taken seriously. Authors who are published through traditional means work hard to perfect their craft and their manuscripts. The books you see on library shelves may well have started life as a manuscript that had many doors closed on it, went back to the author's desk for revision, and were then sent out again to dozens of publishers before being picked up by one.

Some authors will tell you that it's next to impossible to be published in the trade and mass market industry, but you should ask yourself how all those books made it to their places on the shelves of your local library and bookstore. Traditional publication is far from easy; the numbers may be against you, but if you're serious about writing and work hard to make it the best that it can be, it's going to be worth the rejection you're going to face.

The Cost of Self-Publishing

Self-publishing is expensive. Even print-on-demand (POD) methods can cost a pretty penny. For a self-published paperback with a four-color cover and several black and white photos and illustrations, you can expect to pay a short-run printer around $1.50 for a print run of 5,000. This comes out to $7,500. Add that to the cost of the cover design (around $1,800) and typesetting (ranging from $1,000 to $3,000), and your projected cost for a paperback edition falls between $11,300 and $13,600. It will cost more if you want to publish a hardcover edition.

This may sound like a lot of gloom and doom, but it is important that you are aware of the pitfalls, drawbacks, *and* benefits of each path to publication before committing your very precious time and energy to any of them. The more educated you are concerning the world of publishing, and the more honestly you assess your goals and expectations, the greater your chances are of being satisfied and successful in the long run. If you have a thick skin, loads of motivation, dedication, time, energy, expendable capital, are willing to do it all,

and think self-publishing may be right for you, read on for details on what is involved in the process.

Planning Your Book

Your first task as a future self-published writer is to honestly assess your goals. What is it that you want out of the book? Is it a special project you plan to distribute only to friends and family, or do you envision a wider market? If so, how wide? Do you hope to see your book on shelves at local bookstores, county-wide, state-wide, regionally, or even beyond? During the planning stage, feel free to dream big. Then, learn everything you can about what you want to do, and adjust your plans as necessary.

If you are writing the book copy (a short description of your book) yourself, make sure that it represents your book well while also in-

cluding key words associated with your subject. You want to draw in your readers, but you also need to make sure that search engines will rank your book as high as possible—you can do that by including popular keywords. Once you complete the book copy, you must select a title, which should be appealing to the age group you are writing for.

The copy and title are just the beginning. If you are publishing a picture book, a chapter book, or any other work that requires illustrations, you will need to locate the art. Even if your work is a young adult novel that does not require illustrations, there is still the cover art to consider. If you know an artist who is willing to contribute, you may consider discussing your project with them. However, especially if the artist is someone you know, be sure that their work is of the caliber you are seeking before requesting it and before feelings are hurt or reputations are damaged.

Other aspects of planning to consider are the back matter and a possible foreword. Will you use a foreword? It may not be necessary to include unless your book is nonfiction. The back matter is the brief synopsis on the back of the book, which is usually one to three paragraphs long and hits on all the main points in the book. Back matter needs to be succinct, well-written, and it should interest the reader. The back of the book needs to interest a child enough that he or she will beg mom or dad to buy it.

Endorsement blurbs also appear on the back cover, and these are usually one or two positive sentences from someone who has read your book. If your book is a nonfiction picture book about narwhal whales, you may want to query for blurbs from an author who has published children's nonfiction and from an expert in whales. Look at the back matter of at least a dozen different books in the bookstore and compare notes.

Finding Writers, Illustrators, and Editors

The *Literary Market Place* (*LMP*) is a guide to resources for publishers. In the Book Manufacturing section, you can find information on services for art, word processing, printing, and binding. Organizations like the Publisher's Marketing Association and the Small Publishers Association of North America provide services and newsletters to members that can help you locate everyone from editors to typesetters, as well as keep you up to date on events like workshops, fairs, and seminars.

To access this guide, check with your local library or a nearby college or university library to find out if they carry this comprehensive guide in print form or if they are online subscribers. If not, you can visit **www.literarymarketplace.com** to access the guide. Users must register on the site to access a limited version of the guide free of charge, but to access all of it, you must subscribe and pay $24.95 for a one-week subscription, or $399 for a year.

Maybe you feel you have a great idea for a book but have little confidence in your writing skills. Where do you begin? First, get your ideas down on paper, even if the result is disorganized and unpolished. If you're looking for someone else to write the story for you, and you want to provide the raw material, consider a website like Elance (**www.elance.com**).

Elance is a site where professionals sign up to provide services under various categories, including writing and translation, design and multimedia, and web programming. Elance providers take skills tests to qualify their abilities, and they provide services in the writing category such as editing, proofreading, ghostwriting, and children's writing.

If you seek assistance from an editorial or proofreading service, or from an individual, know what it is that your manuscript requires. Do you need a ghostwriter? A proofreader? Someone to consult to find out if you are on the right track and determine whether your work is marketable? You can also seek the services of a professional who will assist you as a writing coach, one-on-one or as part of a workshop, or from someone who will provide a general reading and evaluation of the work. When you determine what you need, ask questions to find out if the editor, proofreader, coach, or writer has experience in children's books. Find out as much as you can about their experience before spending your time and money investing in their help.

Some questions to ask an editor are:

- How will the correspondence take place?

- Is there a charge for consultation and initial evaluation?

- Is there a charge for follow-up questions and feedback?

- Do you provide an overview, such as a general evaluation sheet, in addition to the comments and editing in the manuscript?

- What are the other charges associated with editing the manuscript?

- Do the fees differ for editing revisions?

- Can I contact your previous clients, or can they provide referrals?

- Are there any discounts, such as for SCBWI members?

When looking for an illustrator, try to find one whose style appeals to you and, most importantly, whose artistic skill will bring your story to life. First, check the SCBWI website (**www.scbwi.org**) to look for children's illustrators. The website is also useful for its listings of other professional websites, art colleges, book conferences, and other industry organizations. Look into a variety of sources to find illustrators. Find several illustrators whose work you like, and be prepared to discuss whether they require a flat fee or if they want a royalty deal.

You should definitely have a contract that you both sign to make sure that everyone understands the terms and conditions of the agreement. Remember that the work will be a collaboration, and that your story will sometimes be a lot more successful if you allow the art to replace some of the words you might have written otherwise.

Determining Price

Coming up with a book price isn't the easiest thing, because a lot goes into your book in the first place. Anyone who helps sell your book

receives a percentage of the profit, including bookstores, wholesalers, dealers, and distributors. Then, there are complimentary promotional copies to be sent out to reviewers, which may account for 10 to 20 percent of your total stock. Then, you have to figure in the cost of advertising and returns on damaged stock that is sent back by bookstores.

There's just a lot to think about. Potential buyers want to see a fair price on the book, but the price can also reflect the book's credibility, so make sure you don't underprice your masterpiece.

There are a few formulas for determining the book price: **bottom-up** and **top-down**.

Bottom-up
The bottom-up method takes into account the costs involved in getting the manuscript turned into book form and into the hands of

readers. If printing and shipping mean that each book costs $3 to create, and our **markup**—the amount added to the cost price in order to determine profit—is eight times, then your book will be $24, or $23.95, if you use the common $0.95 method. A book that is even five cents cheaper, at $23.95, seems like it costs a lot less than $24. It's basically a play on psychology.

Take into account how you plan on selling your book. If you are distributing through mail order and bookstores, pricing it at eight times the cost of production is a common bottom-up method. If your book is a children's textbook, price it at around five times more.

Top-down

The top-down method of pricing is basically looking at what every-one else is doing. How much are other books like yours selling for in the bookstore? As a general guideline, average the prices of five or ten comparable books and set your price in the middle.

ISBNs and Barcodes

An International Standard Book Number (ISBN) is a measure of inventory and identification that is issued to each individual book for shipping purposes. Different editions of the same book receive differ-ent ISBNs.

An ISBN is acquired through ISBN.org by Bowker—**www.isbn. org**—where you will also find price listings. The numbers are avail-able for purchase in blocks of 10, 100, and 1,000. The ISBN website posts a recommendation that publishers purchase enough ISBNs to last them for five years. This is for a few reasons. The more numbers purchased, the less they cost. You will also be able to maintain the same publisher prefix for a longer period of time.

If you require only a single ISBN, they are offered from **http://myidentifiers.com** for $125, or for $150 with a barcode. Once you start scaling up, the prices start to go down pretty significantly. For example, if you buy 100 ISBNs, you pay $575, which averages out to around $5 per ISBN. The largest offering is 1,000 ISBNs, which costs $1,500 and averages out to about $1.50 for a single ISBN.

If you have ever looked at an ISBN, you may have noticed that they come in a few different forms: a 10-digit form and a 13-digit form. This is because there are so many new titles and they ran out of ISBNs. Additionally, the current prefix, 978, will soon move to 979. According to the ISBN website, the "X" that appears at the end of the number stands in for the number 10; the last number is referred to as a "check digit." The ISBN-13 has five parts: the prefix, group or country identifier, publisher identifier, title or edition identifier, and the check digit.

The barcode represents a translation of the ISBN. Authors or publishers can request barcodes from the ISBN website or from **www.bowkerbarcode.com**. Why invest in a bar code? Most retailers use the bar code for scanning during checkout and sometimes for inventory, and most retailers and wholesalers will not carry your book without a barcode.

If all of this self-publishing stuff is going over your head, it might be a good idea to keep plugging away with submissions to traditional publishers. A lot of people think that self-publishing is easy, and I suppose it can be, but if you want to do things in the best way—in

the most professional, and ultimately the most beneficial way—it can get complicated fast.

There is no shame in trying to get your book published and not giving up. If you need the help of an expert, you might think about getting an agent. The next chapter will walk you through what exactly an agent can offer you and if getting one is your best next step.

CHAPTER 10
Agents

A gents are basically a link between a publisher and an author. Their job is to know everything about the changing world of publishing, such as when an editor changes houses, or any mergers or acquisitions that take place. Agents are connected with editors throughout the publishing industry, and they have an under-

standing of what imprint or house is currently publishing what type of book, who they are publishing, and what they are looking for next. Editors are usually only a phone call away for well-connected agents.

Agents also prepare the submission package. This can be super helpful for you since they already know the following things:

- The publisher's guidelines

- Who wants a query letter

- Who will accept a partial or a full manuscript for review

- Who prefers hard copy format

- Who accepts electronic correspondence

When it comes to contracts, agents help negotiate the best deal for you. Keep in mind that the more money you make, the more the agent makes, so you can make the connection here—they are wholeheartedly rooting for your success. Agents can easily spot a weakness or flaw in a contract or deal. They can also give you insider advice and can let you know when something is industry-standard versus a bit out of the ordinary.

Do You Need One?

Many larger houses will only review new material that comes through an agent. This isn't to be snobby or anything—it just helps the business run much more smoothly. Agented submissions cut down significantly on the materials that editors and readers have to go through to find what works for their house. Good agents know what a publisher wants and what he or she is looking for, so they send more appropriate material than the general public might.

You most likely need an agent if you have a fiction manuscript and want to be published by a larger or mid-sized house. Many agents will only represent authors who have already published a book before. However, it is possible, though rare, to attract a publisher's attention with a query letter. If your letter presents a brief idea of a story that suits their house and is something they would be interested in publishing, they may request to see a partial of your manuscript.

All By Myself

Let's all take a second to sing along with Celine Dion.

Okay, now that that's over, if you're willing to be published by a smaller house, come up with a list of publishers and imprints that accept unsolicited manuscripts. Make sure you're researching the publishers, their recent publications, and their submission guidelines before sending in your work.

If you've written a nonfiction manuscript, you probably won't need an agent. Many agents don't represent authors shopping nonfiction and educational writing.

What to Look For

Like everything else in this book, the biggest piece of advice here is to do your research. Agents usually specialize—some in YA novels, others in picture books. Remember that you might be working with this person for several years (or more). You're also sharing some of your profit, so an agreement you strike between the two of you will last for the life of any contracts signed.

However, it's important to remember that the agent is usually the one who chooses you, not the other way around. Keep in mind that finding an agent can sometimes be even harder than finding a publisher.

But you have to start somewhere, right? When you're coming up with your list of options, look in market guides like the *Children's Writer's and Illustrator's Market* and the online database of the *Society of Children's Book Writers and Illustrators*. Local writer's groups, critique groups, and industry workshops are another great way to get some insider information.

Talk and network with other writers and as many authors as possible. Visit a site like AgentQuery (**www.agentquery.com**) or the Preditors and Editors Literary Agent section at **www.anotherealm.com/prededitors/pubagent.htm** (which also lists warnings against certain agents) to search the database and connect with literary agents. You also might read an article featuring an agent in a publication like *Writer's Digest* or the SCBWI bulletin, for example. You can also consider starting up a LinkedIn profile and doing a bit of networking. While teens usually don't have a need to start a LinkedIn account at such a young age, you're not the norm here. You're a superstar. The world is your oyster.

Making sure the agent is legit
There are a few checkpoints, many of them common sense, that you can use as guidelines to make sure the agent is legit. Start by looking

in the acknowledgements section of several of the agent's client's books. Is the agent mentioned? Can the agent provide references? Talk to several people the agent has worked with to get a broad picture of what it may be like to work with him or her. Below are some other things to keep in mind when looking for an agent.

Fees

Agents usually collect 10 to 15 percent of an advance paid to the author, and 10 to 15 percent of the royalties. Artist's representatives charge between 20 and 35 percent of the royalties, and if foreign rights or movie rights are involved, the percentage will be higher depending on the deal.

Agents who collect fees may be unqualified for their positions or are rip-off artists. Some agents charge authors fees as a source of income when they are not well-connected enough to make a living from commissions. However, agents commonly charge fees to compensate for legitimate costs that are out of the ordinary, such as the retyping of a manuscript, overnight delivery, long distance and out of country calls, and extra copying. Such costs will be made clear up front.

Keep in mind that agents are not editors, and if an agent offers editing services or makes promises to get your work into a certain house for additional fees, they are guilty of disreputable practice.

Memberships and credentials

The *Children's Writers and Illustrator's Market* lists established agents. To become an agent, a person doesn't go through training or certification, but rather becomes an agent through experience, networking, contacts, and asking questions.

Try to find out things such as:

- How long the agent has been in business

- What projects he has worked on

- Whether he has experience with an agency

- If he is with an agency, are there subagents or others specializing in foreign and movie rights?

- Whether he has correspondents overseas or elsewhere, such as Hollywood

- Who will be handling your work and credentials

- Whether he can provide the language (samples) of an author-agency agreement or agency clause for your review

- How correspondence takes place and its frequency

- Method of fund disbursement

- Terms provided for the dissolution of the relationship

Also visit the agent's or agency's website. What information can you find there? Look for things such as:

- Who they have represented

- Who they currently represent

- The experience of the agents

- Submission guidelines (yes, agents have them too)

- The presentation of the site—clean, professional, and informational versus gimmicky and full of hype

- Whether they are members of professional organizations, especially the Association of Authors' Representatives (AAR)

AAR members are required to adhere to a code of ethics and are generally more reputable. For example, members aren't allowed to charge reading fees. You can search on the AAR website for a list of members: **http://aaronline.org/Find**. The equivalent group for illustrators is the Society of Photographers and Artists Representatives (SPAR). Visit **www.spar.org** for more information.

Finding an agent can be a challenge. Generally speaking, agents who are legit won't need to put ads online. Many of those claiming to be agents who have online ads often make their money by charging clients fees, and some are even conduits to self-publishing services. Whatever you decide to do, make sure you fully understand the agreement and are happy with the deal you come up with.

CHAPTER 11

Crafting Your Submission: Query Letters and Submission Packages

A query letter is supposed to thoroughly excite whichever publisher or editor you're trying to reach. It's a replacement for sending an entire manuscript, which is useful because many larger publishers do not accept unsolicited work for review—only material that comes in through agents.

A query letter is a way for you to inform the publisher or editor of the type of book you have to offer. Some publishers may not require query letters, especially for picture books, so if you can send your short picture book manuscript un-agented, do so instead of a query letter, and include a cover letter instead.

Query letters should be short and to the point, and they should describe your book's subject matter, any background information that qualifies you on the subject (especially for nonfiction), and how your book is different from all the others. Query letters require as much attention to professionalism as anything else you send to a publisher. Check the spellings of names and make sure they're paired with the appropriate titles. Nothing would be worse than having your query

letter go through the paper shredder because you misspelled someone's name or had really bad formatting.

Why is it Important?

A query letter is a good way of shopping your manuscript to see who
might be interested. Once you have a list of publishers that are appropriate candidates for your work, the next logical step is to send a
query letter, especially if some of the publishers on that list do not
accept un-agented manuscripts. If you don't have an agent, a query
letter is a way to test the interests of editors. Unlike manuscripts, query
letters can safely be sent out for a single manuscript to many different
publishers at once.

How to Write a Query Letter

Find out a specific editor's name, or the name of the department that
handles the reading. Begin with a salutation, and always err on the side

of professionalism rather than familiarity. Address the editor as Dear Ms. Jones or Dear Pat Jones (if the gender is unclear from the name, use the first and last name). If you are unsure of the gender or can find only a last name, *never* assume the editor is either male or female.

The first paragraph should be your intro. This is where you should try to clutch the editor's attention. Capture her interest, but avoid gimmicks and hard-sell tactics, such as "This manuscript will change your life, and here's why." It's all right to congratulate the editor on any recent successes, but try to come across as genuine in everything you say. After the opener, use the remainder of the paragraph to summarize your book, and do not forget to specify what type of book it is (picture book or YA novel, for example). The summary should be four sentences or less. Close the paragraph by mentioning any enclosures, such as table of contents or an overview, and be sure to state the word count.

The second paragraph should describe your book's audience. You can also include its potential size, which you should boil down to the numbers whenever possible. If your picture book is about a girl who lost her family during a hurricane, mention the number of people whose families were affected by Hurricane X of Year X. This paragraph is also where you can mention a line or imprint that would fit well with your book, how your book is different from the rest, whether your book includes updated information, and whether it's hitting the market at a good time right now and why.

The third paragraph is where you will include your credentials, experience related to the book, professional publications in the subject area, and related education and hobbies. Be sure to include only information that is pertinent to the subject matter and theme of your book.

The final paragraph should close the letter. You can thank the editor for his time and consideration and mention other materials (like the manuscript or sample chapters) that are available upon request. There is no need to reiterate any contact information you have included in the header, but do mention additional ways you can be contacted if there are any.

Avoid These Common Mistakes

First impressions are important. Since your query letter is representing you and your book, you better make sure that thing is spotless. Here are some mistakes you should avoid at all costs:

- Poor spelling

- Grammar and syntax errors

- Faxed query letter or manuscript

- Not including a self-addressed stamped envelope (SASE)

- Wordiness or awkward wording

- Unusual formatting that might come across as attention-seeking, such as decorated or multi-colored envelopes

- Sending a marketing plan (the publisher handles this)

- Folded, creased, badly photocopied, or stained paper

If you avoid these common mistakes, you're one step ahead of the competition.

Preparing the Submission Package

Send your materials in a manila envelope, either folded in a 5- by 7-inch envelope or, for longer manuscripts, 9- by 10-inch. As a gen-

eral guideline, don't fold anything longer than 10 pages; more than 10 pages should go in the large manila envelope. To keep the envelope and its contents from being bent or damaged, place a piece of cardboard inside.

Keep the pages loose and unstapled, or at the most, attach them with a paper clip. Don't use plastic sleeves or report binding. Mail documents longer than 100 pages in a mailing box. Check submission guidelines to find out whether disks are accepted for submissions — this can be a convenient and cost effective way to submit, especially for longer works. Always include a SASE.

Do not send photography, artwork, or illustrations with your manuscript. Publishers want to see the text manuscript only, and if they are interested in your book, they will find the artwork themselves. The text must be strong enough to warrant publication, and it won't be made better by illustrations—it has to stand out on its own. If you're a writer and an illustrator, send several sketches and a finished piece of art (never send originals).

Keep track of what you send and where you send it in a special folder. Create a document or spreadsheet to keep a record of the date you sent the package, what was sent (query letter, proposal, manuscript), where you sent it, and the date and outcome of the response. Make sure you're staying on top of this—it can be extremely useful in the future. Not only can you keep track of where you have shopped your manuscript, but you'll save yourself the embarrassment of sending out duplicates.

Cover letters

The cover letter can follow the basic format, paragraph by paragraph, as a query letter. Provide an overview of your book that highlights the topic, theme, target audience, and any special experience, background, or insight you might have concerning the book. Include any resources you might have that will set your book apart from others in its genre, or anyone you might have interviewed for the book who is an expert in their field.

Be sure to address the letter to an editor, check the spelling of the person's name, check his or her title and address for accuracy, and include your contact information. Be enthusiastic—excitement is contagious! See Appendix 1 for sample cover letters.

Overview and synopsis

If a publisher's guidelines require an overview, know that it is simply a book summary, usually one to three paragraphs in length. An overview hits all the key points of a book, and it might be found on the back cover of a book or in the jacket flap. A synopsis will include a summary of the entire book, and it includes synopses of individual chapters. These can be two to five sentences in length, and can cover the most essential elements, approaches, topics, or themes in each chapter. See Appendix 1 for a sample overview.

Proposals

A proposal — a thorough overview of a book that is not yet written — is usually required for nonfiction work. A proposal may include an outline with a table of contents and chapter summaries, one to three sample chapters, and a bibliography. Proposals are useful for presenting your book as you envision it will be when it is completed, and for showing its organizational structure. Usually, a query letter is sent out first, and for nonfiction especially, an editor may request to see a proposal if she is interested.

Proposals can be 10 to 15 pages long. They should have 1-inch margins and should be double-spaced (but check the publisher's guidelines for specific formatting requirements). A full-length proposal might consist of the overview, a marketing plan describing the target audience, a promotion including how you plan to participate in the book's marketing and publicity, an analysis of competing titles, a book introduction, chapter summaries, sample chapters, and supplementary materials, such as appendices or multimedia. See Appendix 1 for a sample proposal.

Sample chapters

The purpose of sample chapters, usually submitted with proposals, is to show the editor or publisher how awesome you are at writing. If your work is nonfiction, you might want to send the first chapter, as well as one or two additional chapters that showcase excellent writing, interesting facts, useful information, or up-to-date content. If it's fiction, send the first several chapters to draw the editor into the story.

Before you send anything out, it's really important that you double and triple-check your work for spelling errors, grammatical correctness, and factual accuracy. Format the chapters as you would the manuscript, with 1-inch margins. Format a title page, single-spaced, with your name, address, phone number, and email address in the upper left corner. The word count should appear in the upper right hand corner. Center the title halfway down the page, with your double-spaced byline beneath it. See Appendix 1 to refer to the formatting for sample chapters.

Storyboards and book dummies

Storyboards aren't usually submitted with the manuscript, but they're more useful for the author or author-illustrator's personal planning stages. However, if you're an author-illustrator and your book is picked up for publication, be prepared to discuss storyboarding and the layout of the text and illustrations with an art director at some point.

A picture book dummy, the purpose of which is to stand in for a picture book, is submitted with the package (be sure to mention it as an inclusion or enclosure in the cover letter). Don't send original finished artwork, but do make quality color copies. See Appendix 1 for a sample storyboard and book dummy.

Hello From the Other Side

Okay, this time we'll take a brief pause to sing some Adele.

All right, we're back. What exactly happens to your manuscript when you send it out? An average figure for unsolicited manuscripts coming in to a medium-sized house may be around 3,000 per year. You might have heard the term "slush pile." Especially in large publishing houses, it refers to the body of manuscripts that are sent in unsolicited. Top-priority is given, of course, to agented submissions and anything an editor requests.

Typically, an intern or staff member of a publishing house has the job of sorting, opening, and logging in the manuscripts. They don't typically acknowledge the receipt of manuscripts, but if you send a self-addressed stamped postcard, you may receive an acknowledgement.

The reading process usually involves several pairs of eyes passing over your work to determine whether it's worth moving forward. If it makes the cut, it's sent up the chain. Anything containing spelling errors, grammatical mistakes, manuscripts that are essentially a (thinly) disguised imitation of another work, or something that isn't right for the house won't make it. Many houses will also immediately reject anything that doesn't follow their guidelines.

Work that shows promise will often receive a written report and will eventually make its way to an editor's desk. If the editor approves, he will pitch the manuscript to the acquisitions or editorial committee. Only very rarely does an editor have the final say in a manuscript's approval.

Remember that competition is stiff, and that publishers receive a *ton* of submissions from writers hoping to be published. A good majority of submissions show promise and could be profitable with some editorial attention and lovin'.

But publishers do not have the time or ability to take the risk on works that *might* make it. With so much coming in, only those manuscripts that truly stand out will receive a contract.

CASE STUDY: LISA J. MICHAELS

Lisa's portfolio website
URL: www.ljmichaels.weebly.com
Lisa' blog site:
http://theartofpicturebooks.com
Email address: wscribbles@att.net

One primary difference between illustrating for children and illustrating for adult printed media is that printed media for adults usually only requires "spot" images, which is a single illustration to represent/sell a product or represent a company, like a logo or website banner. In relation to books, illustrators only do covers or book jackets for adult novels. There are seldom interior illustrations as opposed to children's books, where illustrations are placed throughout the pages and are every bit as important as the written text. There is also a huge difference in earning potential for illustrators who do adult literature. In the children's lit field, book and magazine cover illustrations usually earn only half as much.

I have heard it said over and over that it is equally hard to find an agent as it is to find a publisher. I think that is definitely true for the new artists just getting started, and I also think it's a blessing for them. There is so much to learn in this business before an illustrator can really be ready for success. If it comes too early, you can make huge mistakes that remain "out there" for everyone to see and reflect back on years down the road. It can be quite embarrassing.

Once you begin working with other illustrators through the critiquing process, most illustrators evolve into much better artists. When I look back on earlier work, I am relieved that my older children's book illustrations were never published. It is not that my work was bad; it is just that I have grown so much since then. You want editors, art directors, and the public to see your work at its best.

It is a good idea to hang around for a while, professionally pursue other illustrators, and find out who's who. Get good advice from the professionals who are willing to share, find out what editors are looking for, and build your portfolio based on that information. Today's illustrator needs to be technologically savvy and able to deliver their end product in a multitude of ways, as each publisher requires different methods. You also need to be able to self promote, as in maintaining a website, blog, Twitter account, Facebook page, and so on.

Once you have all these things in place, only then may it be the time to consider an agent. You will have become more educated about what they should be doing for you, and that could keep you from becoming prey for unscrupulous characters. Educating yourself in the business *before* seeking an agent, and creating a unique image for yourself, will make reputable agents more inclined to view you as "hot property," ripe for the picking.

Concerning the submission process for children's illustrators, make sure you have an excellent cover letter on top of your promotional package. Take the time to find out *exactly* what should (and should *not*) be said. Know *exactly* the right way to format your letter. It is the first thing the editor sees, and it is comparable to walking into his office in a nice dress suit instead of jeans and a T-shirt. It's your first impression, and if it's not impeccable, it will be your last. The competition is stiff.

Second, do not be sloppy. Your package presentation tells the editor just how highly you value your own work. If you don't, why would he or she? If you can't afford to print your samples on high-gloss paper, then use inexpensive plastic sleeves over your work to protect it from the editor's fingerprints and coffee splatters.

Remember that your work could be passed from one editor's desk to the other (getting separated from your package), so make sure that each piece has your name and contact info on the back — otherwise it may get lost along with your chances of being published.

And last, make sure that you give the editor what he or she is yearning for: your own personal style, samples of drawings containing young children, and samples of one child at several different angles (to prove you can carry your character through a whole picture book). Include pieces that show you are capable of creating a background "world" for your characters, both indoors and out.

A dummy book is an important part of the submission package, because it shows the editor and art director that you understand composition, text placement, page turns, and the total construction of a book from start to finish. It displays your ability to create continuity of characters (your character should look like the same person throughout the book), which is difficult and often overlooked by new, inexperienced illustrators.

The ability to construct an excellent dummy book is proof that you have done your homework and that you're ready for a professional assignment. A ton of money goes into the production of picture books, which is why each publisher limits the amount they publish each year. They must choose illustrators wisely to make sure that their investment pays off. Their jobs depend on it.

Although dummy books are important, and you should be able to construct one, they are not an absolute necessity for a submission package. Many illustrators send samples only. If you choose this method, include at least two to three pages from a single dummy book to show character continuity along with some spot illustrations and a post card. Do not expect the post card to be returned, as the editor may want to keep it on/near the desk as a reminder (if he or she likes your work).

Send the publisher samples that are no larger than 8.5-inch by 11-inch. This will fit neatly into the file folder, which will most likely hold your samples for future consideration. Each time you mail in an updated postcard or sample sheet, it will be added to your personal file until they have a project that is right for you. Never think that an editor who keeps your submission package is rejecting you. Sometimes, it takes a while for *your* project to come along. Keep sending updates every four to six months, and the editors will know you are still working and interested. It will give you a leg up over other illustrators who submit only once.

I have not made a lot of money as an illustrator, but I am more fortunate than most people. I get to chase my dream every day. I get to set the pace. I get to pave my own way and search for the right people to help me get where I want to be — where I *need* to be. I breathe life into written words and create worlds where there once was a vast emptiness. I can honestly say that I have been instrumental in helping new authors and illustrators find *their* way through the maze that is the publishing industry, and there is great satisfaction in that. Knowing that you have given back even more than you received is a great feeling of accomplishment and pride. Not to mention, I have made life-long friends along the way. Who could ask for more than that?

Illustrator, Author, and Artist, Lisa J. Michaels travels throughout her native state of Florida conducting illustration workshops for young and old alike. She participates in fine art shows, mentors other illustrators, and produces illustrations for her growing list of clients. She is a member of the nationally known Society of Children's Book Writers & Illustrators (SCBWI), The Florida Publishers Association, The Visual Storyteller's Studio (VSS), The Picture Bookie Showcase, and much more.

Published books illustrated by Lisa include: "My Love," "The Legend of the Eagle Feather," "Robbin, The Girl Who Didn't Want to Practice," "When Mommy Got Cancer," "Me and My Hot Dog Pillow," "The Inner Light," "Sweet Tomatoes," "Big Feats," "Come Fish With Me," "Alphey Loves Letters," "I Want to be Just Like Jesus Too," and the soon to be released "Crawfish Stew."

In 2007, Lisa took second place in the national ABC Children's Picture Book Competition, and her work was featured in Flavor & Fortune Magazine. In 2008, she won first place in the national Dragonfly Publishing Children's Cover art Contest. In 2014, she won the Florida Authors and Publishers Association Gold Medal for cover design, and the Living Now Book Award for picture book illustration.

In addition, Lisa is the developer and moderator of her own online children's book writer's critique group. With 25 members, The Yellow Brick Road is now in its seventh year running, a rare accomplishment in the children's book publishing industry. Over 75 writers have shared their journey through YBR, many of whom are now published authors.

CHAPTER 12

Becoming a Pro: Networking and Promoting Yourself

O ne of the most important parts of being an author is promoting yourself. Sure, writing the book was a pretty big feat, but who cares if there's just a huge cardboard box of unsold books chillin' in your basement?

You need to become a pro in order to find success in the publishing industry. This chapter is going to cover all the bases—you'll learn the basics of networking and how to get started with PR. Let's begin.

Networking as an Author/Illustrator

The word "networking" can be pretty intimating, especially if you've never had a reason to start. You've probably heard of LinkedIn, the social networking site for businesses and business-people, but why would you need one at this point in your life? Well, if you plan on doing some networking as a budding author, it might be a good idea to start thinking about these things.

Get some business cards

It sounds strange—I'm a teen, and I should have a . . . business card?—but it really is a good place to start. Nothing adds legitimacy to your work more than a well-designed business card. This handy little networking tool can include the URL for whatever website or blog you're using to promote your work.

Here are some good business card options:

- Vista Print (**www.vistaprint.com**): Business card options starting at $7.99 for 100 cards.

- Overnight Prints (**www.overnightprints.com**): Business cards priced at $14.45 for 100 premium business cards, but quick delivery is their strength.

- GotPrint.net (**http://gotprint.net**): Simpler business cards that cost around $16 for 100 cards.

Vista Print is probably the most widely used option—this is the one I would recommend for a beginner on a budget.

Stay in tune with children's lit

Staying on top of what's going on in the children's lit world can really work to your advantage when it comes to networking. Consider doing some online surfing and just emailing authors and illustrators you admire. Let them know what you're working on, and ask if they have any advice. They may never respond, but you know what they say: it doesn't hurt to ask.

Check online for competitions or contents that you can enter, too. You might consider saving up a monthly budget for stuff like this — it can really help you to have an award or two under your belt.

You might also consider subscribing to some newsletters and/or magazines — anything that has to do with writing, literature, or publishing will be useful to you. Being thoroughly engrossed in your craft will keep your mind in the right place, and often times, these kinds of things feature agents, authors, and editors, which can be a great resource for you.

Here are some of my favorites:

- Writer's Digest (**www.writersdigest.com**)

- Poets & Writers (**www.pw.org**)

- Children's Book Insider (**http://cbiclubhouse.com**)

- Daily Writing Tips (**www.dailywritingtips.com**)

- The Morning Nudge (**www.morningnudge.com**)

- Helping Writers Become Authors (**www.helpingwritersbecomeauthors.com**)

- Publisher's Weekly (**http://publishersweekly.com**)

- Digital Book World (**www.digitalbookworld.com**)

Go to conferences

Attend conferences if you can (bring along those business cards), and talk to plenty of people in the children's publishing industry. SCBWI offers conferences and workshops to members on a regular basis. Check the organization's website for national and regional events. Also, check the most current copy of the *Children's Writers and Illustrator's Market*, which includes a comprehensive section called "Conferences and Workshops."

When you attend a conference on children's publishing, you don't want to be throwing your manuscript and cover letter at people. Your goal at these types of events is to exchange contact information so that you can follow up in an appropriate amount of time. When you follow up, it helps to mention your meeting at the conference.

CASE STUDY: SARAH S. BRANNEN

Author and Illustrator
www.sarahbrannen.com

My first book was published about seven years after I began devoting most of my time to writing and illustrating for children. In all that time, I had learned as much as I could about the art and craft of children's books. I read hundreds of picture books, took a course at a local museum, attended conferences, joined critique groups, and submitted several dummies that I wrote and illustrated.

After about three years, I was fortunate enough to sign with an agent, and I got my first offer from G. P. Putnam's Sons through her a few months later. Shortly afterward, I was asked to illustrate a book for Charlesbridge Publishing, so I was very busy for the next nine months, doing sketches and finished art for two trade picture books.

As *Uncle Bobby's Wedding*, my book with Putnam, neared publication, I was well aware that I knew almost nothing about book promotion. I had a lot to learn, and I am still learning.

It seems that each publisher handles promotion differently. In some houses, the marketing department works directly with authors. At Putnam, the book's editor coordinates almost everything between the author and the various marketing and publicity departments. My editor was always helpful in answering questions, and he often called or sent an email with suggestions. I went to workshops on marketing and self-promotion and asked around as much as possible.

Because my book has a specialized market, the gay parenting community, I needed to spend a lot of time gathering information about media markets. Putnam backed me up, paying for the postcards I had printed, along with the postage, and they were great about sending books to all the names I came up with. For the most part, I set up bookstore and media appearances myself.

I'm still learning about conference appearances and what role the publisher plays to help them happen. I sent out a huge postcard mailing to coincide with the publication date for *Uncle Bobby's Wedding*, mostly to gay organizations and media, but also anyone I thought might be interested in same-sex weddings, like Unitarian Universalist churches.

To promote my book, I:

- Emailed gay-family bloggers, and, if they responded, had Putnam send them a book. Most of them responded and many wrote blogs about the book. Contacted all the organizations I could find that support same-sex marriage and gay parents.

- Redesigned my website to promote the book as much as possible.

- When invited, I appeared at library and children's writing conferences. I will be speaking at the ALA's Banned Books Week in Chicago in September.

- Set up several local bookstore appearances. When I traveled to San Francisco, I arranged a bookstore and television appearance there.

- Tracked the book online, following up every mention. I found a lot of reviews this way and also some negative blog posts and message board discussions. I also found a video that some kids made, where the book was acted out with stuffed animals.

- When I started to hear about challenges to the book, I contacted the American Library Association's Intellectual Freedom Office, and we have stayed in touch, sharing news about further challenges.

If you are an aspiring author who also illustrates, the first step is to read hundreds of recently published picture books. Analyze them, see what works, get an idea of what is being published these days, and learn what kind of books different houses publish.

- Read and study Uri Shulevitz's *Writing with Pictures.* [For a resource with an up- to-date color section, see *Designer's Guide to Color* by I. Shibukawa and Y. Takahashi.]

- Go to conferences, and join critique groups. As both an author and illustrator, you will need to attend workshops in both writing and illustrating, and you will probably want to join both a writers' group and an illustrators' group.

- Check out **www.yellapalooza.com**. I founded the site along with some good friends. It is the only site we know of devoted to people who both write and illustrate. There are some great message boards and LISTSERVs out there; we have links to all of them on Yellapalooza.

- Join the Society of Children's Book Writers and Illustrators (SCBWI). It is a great resource.

Usually, when I am writing and illustrating a book, I think about the text and the illustrations simultaneously. Sometimes, the first idea for a book is an image. However, *Uncle Bobby's Wedding* was different. Because the subject matter was controversial, it needed to be handled delicately. I rewrote the story from scratch many times before I started thinking about the illustrations. I didn't even realize I was going to illustrate it with animals instead of people until I was refining the final draft.

The first step was to get the text to a final, finished version. My editor, Tim Travaglini, spent some time on this, and we worked on it together. After that, I did a thumbnail dummy, and then the final dummy. Most of the comments on the sketches came from Cecilia Yung, the art director. She and Tim certainly looked at them together, but Cecilia gave me more direction on the art. That said, neither Tim nor Cecilia asked for many changes. They were both completely committed to my vision of the book. Tim and I have continued to work closely on promoting and marketing the book. We get in touch every few weeks.

Sarah S. Brannen is the award-winning illustrator of over fifteen books for children. She is the author and illustrator of Madame Martine (Albert Whitman & Co.), Madame Martine Breaks the Rules (Whitman), and Uncle Bobby's Wedding (G. P. Putnam's Sons). Uncle Bobby's Wedding received extensive publicity upon publication; it was the eighth most-challenged book in the U.S. in 2008.

Sarah also illustrated Feathers: Not Just For Flying, the 2015 Crystal Kite Award winner and an ALA notable book; At Home in Her Tomb, A Junior Library Guild selection; The Fox and the Grapes; The Pied Piper of Hamelin; The Very Beary Tooth Fairy; The Pig Scramble; The Ugly Duckling; The ABC Book of American Homes; Digging for Troy: From Homer to Hisarlik; as well as several other books. She illustrated the 40th Anniversary edition of All Kinds of Families by Norma Simon.

*As a journalist and photographer, Sarah is a regular contributor to Skating Magazine and **www.icenetwork.com**. She has been writing and illustrating children's books since 2001.*

PR and You

You did everything you had to do to get that book done. You're a rock star. The problem is, no one knows you're a rock star except for you and your parents.

People need to find out about your book, and that's where publishers usually come in. Publishers promote books through their usual channels, but authors are also expected to participate in the marketing of their books—this is sometimes even included in the contract.

If you're serious about hitting the market with a boom, you should think about setting up a PR campaign. The following are some ideas for things to add to such a campaign.

School visits

School visits can be really fun, but they aren't necessarily for everyone. If you're not comfortable speaking to a group of children, you can set aside this option and promote your book with other methods. On the other hand, if you can generate excitement about math,

science, history, or reading, then a school visit may be a good avenue for you.

If you choose to do school visits, set up an honorarium (a fee) that you are comfortable with. Often, this is $250 to $400 for an hour-long presentation for a beginning author; as you become more experienced, you can charge more. When setting the honorarium, consider your travel and room and board expenses as well as the budget of the school. Since you're a new author, you might find it useful to set the money aside and focus on getting your name out there.

If you have a website or blog, it may not be a good idea to list your honorarium, as it can scare away potential clients. There are ways to defray costs, such as selling copies of your book that you purchase at a discount from the publisher and staying overnight with a "host family" instead of in a hotel. The key is to entice potential visits by posting what you have to offer.

Contact schools in your area and let them know about your book and what you have to offer. You might even think about meeting with someone at the school (call ahead of time) to drop off promotional and informational materials.

Materials should include the following:

- Information about your book

- An overview of what you plan to do during your visit

- Any supplementary materials, such as handouts, book reviews, and fliers

You can do the same thing with public libraries. Alternatively, prepare a promotional package and mail it out to area schools; follow up with a phone call. Visit children's author Aaron Shepard's website to see more information on how to go about scheduling appearances (**www.aaronshep.com/appearances**).

Book events and signings

Book signings are a much bigger draw when an event is planned around the signing. Contact both independent and chain bookstores, and ask if they host events. Larger bookstores will most likely have a PR manager or community relations coordinator who handles author events and deals with the media. The community, PR, or marketing coordinator is a busy person who is often out in the field. If you have to leave a message, be clear, and try not to ramble on. Leave your book title, the ISBN number, and mention that you will send a press release. Then, fax or mail one, and wait for a response. If you haven't heard anything back in two weeks, follow up with another call. Of course, always be polite and professional.

When you have the chance to speak with the appropriate person, ask about a reading, book party, or publicity event. A book party for your historical middle grade novel might include making treats that children would have loved during the time your novel takes place. Or, for your picture book about a pig princess, it could be a princess-themed reading and event.

Consider the possibilities in incorporating your book into events held regularly by bookstores, such as story times and readings by store facilitators; series club events, such as *American Girls* clubs; and character visits, such as Arthur or Clifford. Once you have determined what you would like to take place at the event, how will you advertise it? Will you put together a press release and send it to the local media? Are you willing to spend money on advertising? Let the PR coordinator know how you plan to spread the word, and she will be more willing to participate in advertising, too.

Visit bookstores in your area and offer to autograph copies of your books. Sales associates can place an "autographed" sticker on the books (which sometimes sell for a higher price, especially for well-known authors), and it can place them in high-visibility areas near the cash register, on displays, and in the store windows.

Do this before or after a signing or event, or simply drop by a bookstore the next time you're passing by, and ask if they carry copies of your book. If so, offer to sign them. If not, bring a copy of your book along and encourage the manager to order it. Allow the manager to keep a complimentary copy to keep the title fresh in his mind for the next time he or his staff places orders. You can encourage librarians to order copies by doing the same thing.

Book tours

Okay, so maybe this isn't really on your radar right now, but it's something to think about. Book tours are usually arranged by the publisher for those certain authors whose books sell in the hundreds of thousands of copies. However, because of cost, publishers usually spring for tours only when the author has an established track record of such successes under his belt.

As an author that's new to the publishing game, your best option is to decide if it's even worth the cost and effort. Many authors who go on tours keep them brief or relatively close to home. Also, be on the lookout for book fairs where you can set up a table.

Keep holidays in mind, like Halloween, National Children's Book Week, and famous author or historic figures' birthdays, like Dr. Seuss or Benjamin Franklin. Do what you can to promote your book, and the publisher will help you by letting you know of any upcoming events. Do not expect them to assist with expenses if you're a new author, but if it happens, you can appreciate it all the more.

Also, keep in mind that you, as a published children's author promoting your book, are news. Don't be afraid to spread the good news to local media stations or radio hosts when you're giving a tour, a talk, or are engaging in any sort of promotion for your work.

Radio and television interviews

Before contacting a radio station, try to find out what shows they run and whether any relate to the topic of your book. Most radio stations have websites, so start by looking online for their scheduling and programs. Whether for radio or television, try to come up with a "hook" that's newsworthy, timely, informational, or that relates both to current events and to your book or topic.

If your book takes place in a certain place, contact stations in that area. They will likely be interested in helping to promote a published work of local interest. Your role on the show will be more along the lines of talent or entertainment, so promote your interesting or unique idea rather than an overt book promotion. You'll have a chance to plug your book, but the hook is what will keep viewers viewing and listeners listening.

Contact local television stations and pitch your idea to them. Your primary concern should be, before contacting any media outlet, researching their target audience. Especially as a writer for children, your category may be considered niche to some stations or media outlets. Be sure you can pitch your idea to meet their interests and their audience's needs. Just as you target publishers before submitting your material, do the same when pitching your hook to the media.

On air, be yourself, and stay focused on your topic. Be prepared for chitchat and banter, and prepare ahead of time for what you want to say. Be flexible, and prepare to work your comments in at a different angle than you may have anticipated. Bring a copy of your book with you to the show, and mention any events or readings, and when and where they will be. After the taping, send a thank-you note.

CASE STUDY: KATHRYN STARKE

Urban Literacy Specialist, Author, and Founder/CEO of Creative Minds Publications, LLC
www.creativemindspublications.com

Thanks to social media, this is the best time for a writer of all ages to be showcased, recognized, and even published. Everyone has a story to tell, and self-publishing platforms now allow us to share our stories with a broad audience. In the traditional publishing industry, agents and distributors are still invaluable. Well-written books still become best sellers and receive awards. However, promoting yourself and showcasing your work can get you the recognition, sales, and press you deserve.

I wrote my first children's book, *Amy's Travels*, when I was teaching second grade. I sent my manuscript to a local publisher in Richmond, Virginia, who loved my story but didn't publish children's books at the time. He was willing to serve as packager and printer of my book, so (with a push from my entrepreneur father), I started my own business. As authors, we have the tendency to think our book is amazing. Unfortunately, numbers don't lie. When the first printing of 1500 books of *Amy's Travels* were sitting in my apartment, I knew I had to take action. They were not going to move themselves. This is where the PR comes in.

Since I was an elementary school teacher, I reached out to librarians and teacher friends asking to share my book with their school. I was a guest author for book fairs, reading nights, and book store signings. I sent out emails every single day locally, nationally, and internationally to educators, stores, conferences, and media out lets. I was asked to speak at literacy conferences and was interviewed on local television news stations and national radio stations. I created a website, started a blog, and used social media to my advantage.

Just like we write for a specific audience, we have to target a particular audience in marketing as well. I initially wrote my children's book for teachers to use in their classrooms to teach the seven continents. I brainstormed all of the possible connections for *Amy's Travels*, and I shared the story behind the book with bilingual schools, travel agencies, and multicultural blogs. My book was recommended as a multicultural text by the California Department of Education and was added to Amazon. Knowing that teachers and moms are huge buyers of children's books, I shared every review, article, and link about *Amy's Travels* on Pinterest, Facebook, LinkedIn, and Twitter.

Ten years after publishing my very first children's book, I can say that *Amy's Travels* is in its second edition, third printing, and is used in homes on over 20 countries on 6 continents. My company has expanded by publishing other children's books and educational resources all written by elementary school educators. We offer literacy events at schools and stores, we are planning a book tour for a brand new title, and we continue to share work with cherished and brand new followers on social media. This can happen for anyone willing to work, anyone that is determined, and anyone that can creatively think of ways to always introduce your work to someone new.

The great thing about books, especially children's books, is they never go out of style, and there is always a new reader you need to introduce your work to.

*Kathryn Starke is an urban literacy specialist, author, and founder/ CEO of Creative Minds Publications, LLC, a literacy educational company. Like her Facebook page (**www.facebook.com/creativeminds publications**) and follow her on Twitter, Instagram, and Pinterest— @KathrynStarke—to learn more about writing and publishing.*

Conclusion

We have crossed a lot of territory through the course of this book. You know why you should write for kids, you're familiar with the different kinds of children's books you can create, you have some beginning knowledge about the children's book publishing industry, and you're starting to get the hang of the writing and revision process. Oh, and how could I forget about the marketing stuff?

I dare say that you are on your way to becoming an expert. But don't let your quest for knowledge and betterment stop here. Use the resources and suggestions in this book to keep moving forward. You've heard this upwards of probably 20 times now, but seriously—if you had to take one thing away from this book, it should be that in order to be a successful writer of any kind, **you need to read**.

So, before you start crafting up your work of art, spend some time with your nose in a book, make the library your new evening

hang-out, and let your brain soak up the wonder that is children's literature. Before you know it, you'll be taking selfies with your fresh-off-the-press masterpiece.

Go get 'em.

Afterword

've always had a passion for writing. In elementary school, we had the opportunity to write a book, and I wrote a book about shoes and one about buses. When I became a teen, I embraced music and poetry. In college, I took creative writing and had to write 40 poems for one assignment. Throughout my twenties, I continued to write poetry as a hobby, and into my thirties, I strived to take things to the next level.

The next step was writing a book, and I decided it would be a children's book. When writing, I went through a creative process. The book came piecemeal. I worked on this while working a full-time job, so I didn't put a time frame on the process, but I did try to set some goals. You can't force creativity. Whenever you have a creative idea, always record it, so you don't forget the thought. As my ideas flowed, I would write them down, and soon, I created a storyline. I chose a ladybug as the main character, because they symbolize happiness. They are also considered "lucky."

I worked on this project for around five years. I had to find an illustrator and decided that I wanted to self-publish. I realized it was important to possess passion, perseverance, preparation, and patience in this lengthy process. I could envision what I wanted this to look like as a final product, but I knew it would take time, money, and many resources to make this come to fruition. In 2015, I self-published my book, *Lucky Little Ladybug*, on Createspace.

The book includes activity pages, because I envisioned the book being interactive for kids, to not only encourage literacy, but to offer additional learning tools as well. The book is for ages 3-7. The message of the book is to emphasize that we are all unique and individual in our own way. I believe that teaching kids this positive message is valuable in many ways, including building self-esteem. The book was recently listed on Pacer's website, a national anti-bullying organization, as well. My book is online in a paperback and Kindle version.

I'll never forget the joy of seeing my book for the first time and holding it. It was an idea that became a reality!

So You Want To Write A Children's Book: A Step-By-Step Guide to Writing and Publishing for Kids has touched on all the important ideas when deciding to write a children's book—the creative and technical process, information regarding the publishing industry, and much more. When making the decision to write a children's book, the first question to ask yourself is what/who inspires you? When thinking of a topic, do you have an important message to share? What interests you? Would you like to write as a hobby or would you like to create a business?

From concept to completion, there is a lot to consider. What may work for one person may be different for another. Once you've made the decision to write a book, creating an outline of your goals is helpful. Utilize all resources available, including libraries, and possibly contact creative writing students at colleges for advice. Also contact established authors to mentor you and to possibly offer information regarding publishing.

You can also look for internships that relate to writing and publishing to learn more about the process. Look online or in your community for other teen writers. If your strength is writing but not illustrating, there are many resources to identify an illustrator. Many colleges have art students, and they may be interested in working with you on a book.

You may start with writing a children's book and become interested in writing all genres. I'm currently working on an inspirational quote book for adults as well as a business tip book for women and aspiring entrepreneurs. I also have some ideas for future children's books as well. When you're creative, there are many possibilities.

I was just a young girl, doodling in my journals. Now, I'm a published author. You can be too! Whether it be through blogs, magazines, or books, the goal of my writing is to have an inspirational, encouraging, and empowering message. I use my words to have a positive impact. You're fortunate to be in a time where you can reach a large audience with a touch of a button, and you can be a voice for your message. What legacy would you want to leave with kids? What's your story?

Believe in yourself, and know that if you work hard, stay focused, and utilize resources such as this book to create goals and a plan, you can write a book and see it come to fruition. One day, you'll be able to be a mentor with your experience as an established author with the warm pages of a freshly published book in your hands.

—Melissa Carter, debut children's book author

*Melissa Carter is an author, mentor and entrepreneur. Melissa works full-time in marketing and has a wellness business. Melissa also has experience in event planning and fundraising. In her spare time, Melissa enjoys writing, fitness, and enjoying life. For more information, please visit her website (**www.wholisticpackage.com**).*

APPENDIX A
Sample Documents

Storyboard

The storyboard is usually sketched by hand. Illustrations are rough at this stage and serve as an approximation of the final layout.

Sample Artist's Résumé

Include an artist's résumé and business cards with your portfolio. Keep in mind that an artist's résumé typically includes an artist's statement, education, and shows in reverse chronological order, awards, and publications.

Graham Best
P.O. Box 1234
New York, NY 10010
(555) 555-1234
graham@grahamartist.com
Artist's Statement

I am a painter living and working in New York City, New York. My work is a mixture of paintings, prints, and gouache. Drawing on my experience working with children and my use of various materials, I provide a window into children's culture. Shortlisted for the Mercury prize in 2008, my work can be seen in galleries in Los Angeles, New York, and London, as well as online at www.grahamartist.com.

EDUCATION

2008-2011
Massachusetts College of Art and Design, Master of Fine Arts

Studied with Stuart Diamond and Fred Liang. Participated in artist in residency development program. Thesis: Warhol's Continued Influence. Graduated Summa Cum Laude. GPA 3.958.

2004-2008
Massachusetts Institute of Technology, B.A. Double Major: Art and History

Art History/Art Studio. History Specialization: Civil War. Thesis topic combining both majors: Art in the Civil War. Graduated Summa Cum Laude with Distinction in both majors. GPA 3.90, Honors Program.

AWARDS: Alumni Service Scholarship Award and Academic Distinction Scholarship.

EXHIBITIONS

2009
"Black and White Fortress" Wexler Hall Group Show, Boston, MA (October) Curated by Jimmy Franklin

2008
"Civilized America" Dailey Gallery, New York, NY. Contributing artist. (April)
"Refracted Light" Detroit Children's Gallery, Detroit, MI. Collaboration with Amy
Fish. (January)

2007
"Kids in the Audience" Christus Hospital Benefit, Invitational art show and
auction (August)
"Paintings for Children" Critique group, featured in Arts in America.
Blacklight Gallery,
MIT. Invitational Group show (September-December)

REVIEWS & PUBLICATIONS

2009
Catalog for Boston Art Museum

2008
Haverford News. "Children's Artists at Large." October 4, 2008; pp. B3 & B7
Angie Tidwell
Boston Globe. "Images of Myth." August 14, 2008; pp. 14-16. Bruce Stone

AWARDS

2009
Artist in Residency Program, Bruce Hall, Oregon State University. Fall 2008. Stipend
and teaching.
Youth Artists Magazine Best Emerging Artists

2008
Sharon E. Pfister Award for Children's Artists: Movers & Shakers.

2007
Perilous Posters Prize, 2nd place.

MEMBERSHIPS

- SCBWI
- Graphic Artists Guild

Sample Query Letter

Jane Writer
1234 Show-Don't-Tell Lane
Boston, MA 02101

January 1, 20--

Edna Editor
Best Books Ever
1234 Bindery Blvd.
New York City, NY 10010

Dear Ms. Editor,

Our era is one of constantly changing technology and lightning-speed advancements. Today's youth are in an especially exciting position to grow as leaders and innovators in an age where science and invention are some of society's top priorities. My nonfiction picture book about Thomas Edison is uniquely positioned to help young readers understand the creative processes and inventive thinking that drove one of history's greatest inventors.

The Legacy of Thomas Edison: More Than Just the Inventor of the Light Bulb begins with a biography that highlights the dedication, drive, and creative genius that were that hallmarks of the inquisitive young Edison, a person whose insatiable love of learning and invention quite literally changed the world. The book's unique layout includes "Do-It-Yourself" sidebars that will get kids interacting with some of Edison's actual experiments and inventions. The book also endeavors to inspire a love of science and invention by illustrating some of the thought processes of Edison and how he used his problem-solving abilities to create systems and objects that made an impact on our everyday lives.

To date, biographies of Thomas Edison focus on his life or his inventions. To my knowledge, my book is the only one that examines the workings of the inventor's mind as well as his unique creative thought processes, drive, and motivation. Young readers will gain special insight into scientific methodology and will have the opportunity to try some of Edison's experiments for themselves.

As a visual artist with a background in design and layout, I can contribute the art and graphic elements to the book. If you are interested, I can send it to you in completed form in three months. Thank you for your consideration.

Sincerely,

Jane Writer

Sample Cover Letter — When You Are Unpublished

Jane Writer
1234 Show-Don't-Tell Lane
Boston, MA 02101

January 1, 20--

Edna Editor
Best Books Ever
1234 Bindery Blvd.
New York City, NY 10010

Dear Ms. Editor,

Congratulations on your new position at Best Books Ever. I was excited to find out about your new picture book line, and am submitting my book for your consideration. *Jiminy Jumping Jacks!* is the rollicking tale of a young turtle's struggle to live up to the athletic triumphs of his best friends, Rabbit and Fox. Enclosed is my 250-word manuscript.

With an increasing focus on keeping kids healthy, parents, teachers, and librarians will appreciate the values represented in the adventures of the three friends. The book is fun for kids to read and not only shows the importance of eating right and exercise, but also deals with an experience many kids can relate to. For children whose athletic abilities are not quite at the level as those of their friends, participating in sports can be disheartening. Children who are overweight often struggle with body image and feelings of social inadequacy, and turtle's interactions with his friends are taken from real-life examples.

I have taught physical education for 10 years and have seen firsthand the effects that feeling inadequate has on children's self-esteem. Not many children's books address this topic, and I hope that mine can fill a void while showing children that they can turn this difficult situation around through both perseverance *and* fun.

I appreciate your time and consideration in reviewing my manuscript. Enclosed is a SASE for a reply only. This is not a simultaneous submission.

Sincerely,

Jane Writer

Sample Cover Letter — When You Are Published

Jane Writer
1234 Show-Don't-Tell Lane
Boston, MA 02101

January 1, 20--

Edna Editor
Best Books Ever
1234 Bindery Blvd.
New York City, NY 10010

Dear Ms. Editor,

Daisy's Dash is the humorous story of a young prankster who cannot seem to help herself. At school, at the park, at the mall, Daisy pulls pranks wherever she goes — until one day, when she tries to pull a prank on a bigger prankster than herself...

I hope you will enjoy the unique fun and humor of Daisy's story. It shows examples of how to deal with bullies, but in a way that will have young readers laughing.

I am the author of several picture books, including *Mama's Lullaby* and *The Biggest Birthday Bash*. My short stories have appeared in *American Girl* and *Highlights for Children*.

I appreciate your time and consideration in reviewing my manuscript. Enclosed is a SASE for a reply only. I am submitting my manuscript exclusively to you.

Sincerely,

Jane Writer

Sample Proposal

THE LEGACY OF THOMAS EDISON:
MORE THAN JUST THE INVENTOR OF THE LIGHT BULB

By Cynthia Reeser

CHAPTER 1 — THE MIND OF THE YOUNG GENIUS

This chapter discusses the intellectual and creative development of the young Thomas Edison, from the time he was rejected by his teacher to his years in home schooling. Influenced by his mother — who, in his words, "was the making of me" — young Thomas showed an insatiable love of learning and spent many hours training his mind and reciting poetry. Sidebars include some of the young Thomas' experiments.

CHAPTER 2 — A WORLD OF INVENTIONS

This chapter outlines many of Edison's inventions, and how and why the inventor thought them up. Includes an exciting description of Thomas Edison and Alexander Graham Bell's working relationship and how they competed against one another. Discusses communication science as it was then and how Edison's inventions have developed into modern technologies. Includes descriptions of tangible ways that the inventor has influenced contemporary life and what the world would be like without his inventions. Stresses the importance of creative and scientific thinking and includes many detailed, full-color illustrations.

CHAPTER 3 — APPLIED INVENTIONS AND EDISON'S METHODS

With a look at how Edison developed a system for electricity, the phonograph, and many other useful objects, kids learn about Edison's scientific methods and how he put them to practical use. With Edison's methods in mind, readers can try several experiments and inventions themselves. Sidebars are geared to encourage children in thinking scientifically and to help them generate ideas of their own.

Historic Sites

List of Inventions

Books about Thomas Edison

Index

Sample Overview

The Legacy of Thomas Edison:
More than Just the Inventor of the Light Bulb

During his lifetime, Thomas Edison obtained 1,093 patents for his many inventions. He is credited with inventing the light bulb, as well as the phonograph and the carbon transmitter, which made the voices through Alexander Graham Bell's invention — the telephone — audible enough to encourage the device's widespread use. Edison was a dedicated inventor who set up the first research and development laboratory in the world with the establishment of his center in West Orange, New Jersey, in 1887.

This book begins with a biography that highlights the dedication, drive, and creative genius that were that hallmarks of the inquisitive young Edison, a person whose insatiable love of learning and invention quite literally changed the world. This nonfiction picture book's unique layout includes "Do-It-Yourself" sidebars that will get kids interacting with some of Edison's actual experiments and inventions. Designed to educate children on the life of Thomas Edison, the book also endeavors to inspire a love of science and invention by illustrating some of the thought processes of Edison and how he used his problem-solving abilities to create systems and objects that made a difference.

Sample Manuscript — Picture Book

Jane Writer
1234 Show-Don't-Tell Lane
Boston, MA 02101
(555) 555-1234
E-mail: jwriter@janewriter.com

250 words

Jiminy Jumping Jacks!
by
Jane Writer

"BAM!" Rabbit hit the baseball clear across the field.

"Woo hoo!" yelled Fox.

Turtle was nervous. He didn't feel like playing today.

He reached in his shell for some snack cakes.

"You're up, Turtle!" called Fox.

Turtle slowly trudged over to home.

"What's wrong, Turtle?" asked Rabbit. Rabbit was still excited about his hit.

Sample Manuscript — Chapter Book

Amy Kline   35,000 words
1234 Show-Don't-Tell Lane
Boston, MA 02101
(555) 555-1234
E-mail: akline@amyklinewriter.com

The Best Choice
by
Amy Kline

Chapter One

Anne sat at her desk while the teacher droned on about math problems. She didn't "get" math. In fact, it had always been her worst subject. It was not going to get any better this year, she could tell.

"Psst!" Brianna was trying get her attention again. "Psst!"

"What?" Anne snapped, turning around in her seat. Anne had wanted the teacher to think she was paying attention, but Brianna was her best friend and knew better than that. "You're going to get me in trouble!"

"Anne," Mrs. Kendrick said.

Ugh, not again, Anne thought.

"Anne, is talking going to be a problem this year?"

"No, ma'am," Anne sighed. There was no use explaining anything. Brianna would just think she was trying to get her in trouble. Thank goodness she only had one other class with her this year, and that was P.E.

Brianna snickered behind her. Anne couldn't wait for lunch.

She picked up her pencil and tried to pay attention, but she couldn't stop her mind from wandering. There were some kids kicking a ball outside the window. They looked like 6th graders, but she couldn't tell. One of them looked familiar. He was wearing a blue shirt that looked like one her brother used to have.

Sample Author Flier

Jane Writer
Children's Author

> *"A gifted writer… she makes reading to children fun,*
>
> *for adults and kids!"*
>
> **— Harold O'Published, Publication of the Month**

When Jane isn't writing picture books, you can be sure to find her giving presentations at an elementary school somewhere. The award-winning author of *This is My Bus, Jimmy's Magic Day*, and *The Dog that Wouldn't Stop Running*, she is a dedicated and talented writer for children.

Jane has published stories in *Highlights for Children, American Girl, Muse, Cricket*, and *Nick*. When she isn't writing or reading to kids, she loves to go horseback riding and take picnic lunches with her three children.

Jane's work has received awards from the American Library Association and SCBWI. Visit her Web site at www.janewriter.com.

Jane Writer
P.O. Box 1234
Boston, MA 02101
www.janewriter.com

Sample Book Flier

The Legacy of Thomas Edison:

More Than Just the Inventor of the Light Bulb

By Cynthia Reeser

During his lifetime, Thomas Edison obtained 1,093 patents for his many inventions. He is credited with inventing the light bulb, as well as the phonograph and the carbon transmitter, which made the voices through Alexander Graham Bell's invention — the telephone — audible enough to encourage the device's widespread use. Edison was a dedicated inventor who set up the first research and development laboratory in the world with the establishment of his center in West Orange, New Jersey, in 1887.

This book highlights the dedication, drive, and creative genius that were that hallmarks of the inquisitive young Edison, a person whose insatiable love of learning and invention quite literally changed the world. This nonfiction picture book's unique layout includes Do-It-Yourself sidebars that will get kids interacting with some of Edison's actual experiments and inventions. Designed to educate children on the life of Thomas Edison, the book also endeavors to inspire a love of science and invention by illustrating some of the thought processes of Edison and how he used his problem-solving abilities to create systems and objects that made a difference.

"Illuminating ... Reeser shows the creative process behind Thomas Edison the thinker. Kids will love trying the same experiments Edison did as a child."

— Publishers Weekly, 1/1/01

Best Books Ever, 2010, 64 pages, full-color illustrations, LC #12-34567, ISBN 1-234-56789-0, $14.95, Grades 4-8

Sample Review Query

Jane Writer
1234 Show-Don't-Tell Lane
Boston, MA 02101

January 1, 20--

Publication of the Month
Attn: Ricky Reviewer
1234 Bowery Blvd.
New York City, NY 10010

Dear Mr. Reviewer,

My book was recently released from Best Books Ever. I am writing to ask if you would be interested in reviewing it. *Jiminy Jumping Jacks!* is the tale of a young turtle's struggle to live up to the athletic triumphs of his best friends, Rabbit and Fox.

With an increasing focus on keeping kids healthy, parents, teachers, and librarians will appreciate the values represented in the adventures of the three friends. The book is fun for kids to read and not only shows the importance of eating right and exercise, but also deals with an experience many kids can relate to. For children whose athletic abilities are not quite at the level as those of their friends, participating in sports can be disheartening. Children who are overweight often struggle with body image and feelings of social inadequacy, and turtle's interactions with his friends are taken from real-life examples.

I have taught physical education for 10 years and have seen firsthand the effects that feeling inadequate has on children's self-esteem. Not many children's books address this topic, and I hope that mine call fill a void while showing children that they can turn this difficult situation around through both perseverance and fun.

Please let me know if you are interested, and I will gladly send a complimentary review copy your way. Thank you for your time.

Sincerely,

Jane Writer

Sample Review Slip

Best Books Ever Presents for Review

Title: *The Legacy of Thomas Edison: More than Just the Inventor of the Light Bulb*

Author: Cynthia Reeser

Edition: First

Number in Print: 100,000

CIP/LCCN: 1234567890

ISBN: 1-23456-789-0

Pages: 64

Cover art: Illustration by Cynthia Reeser

Price: $14.95

Season: Fall 2010

Publication date: October 2010

Rights:
   a. Subsidiary: Book club, paperback
   b. Syndication

Please send two copies of your review to the address below:

Best Books Ever
Public Relations Department
1234 Bindery Blvd.
New York City, NY 10010
Tel: (555) 555-1234; Fax: (555) 555-2345
Info@BestBooksEver.com
www.BestBooksEver.com

Sample Press Release

FOR IMMEDIATE RELEASE

October 5, 2010

Children's Book Reveals the Importance of Team Sports

Bestselling children's author Jane Writer explores the other side of youth sports in her latest book from Best Books Ever, *Jiminy Jumping Jacks!* Released in October 2010, *Jiminy Jumping Jacks!* is available for $14.95 from Barnes & Noble Booksellers, Borders Books, Amazon.com, and fine booksellers nationwide.

Writer's picture book promises to make an impact on children everywhere who struggle with weight problems. These children often suffer from low self-esteem and feelings of inadequacy, especially when it comes to participating in team sports. While the situation may be grim for a portion of American's population, Writer makes a bleak situation fun and addresses a difficult topic effortlessly. The story of turtle and his friends exhibits a supportive situation that is sure to be a hit with parents, teachers, and children's librarians.

Writer has taught physical education to children for 10 years and has seen firsthand the positive effects of team sports on overweight children. Her program, "Fitness is Fun," has helped more than 75 children reduce their weight and see measurable health benefits. And Writer certainly has an audience — according to a recent study, one out of every three American children is overweight or obese. "Educating children about eating right and the importance of exercise is vital," said Writer. "But children don't have to know that — I hope my book makes it fun for them."

For additional information, contact Netty Networker at (555) 555-1234.

About Jane Writer: The award-winning author of *This is My Bus*, *Jimmy's Magic Day*, and *The Dog that Wouldn't Stop Running*, Jane Writer is a dedicated and talented writer for children. She has published stories in *Highlights for Children*, *American Girl*, *Muse*, *Cricket*, and *Nick*. When she is not writing or reading to kids, she loves to go horseback riding and take picnic lunches with her three children.

CONTACT INFORMATION:

Netty Networker
XYZ PR Firm, Inc.
(555) 555-1234 (voice)
(555) 555-2345 (fax)
netty@xyzpr.com
www.xyzpr.com

Information and Resources

Organizations for Children's Writers and Illustrators

The Authors Guild (**www.authorsguild.org**)

The Children's Book Council (**www.cbcbooks.org**)

Graphic Artists Guild (**www.graphicartistsguild.org**)

The National Writers Union (**www.nwu.org**)

PEN (**www.pen.org**)

Poets & Writers, Inc. (**www.pw.org**)

Publishers Marketing Association (**www.pma-online.org**)

Small Publishers Association of North America (**www.spannet.org**)

Society of Photographers and Artists Representatives (**www.spar.org**)

The Society of Children's Book Writers and Illustrators (SCBWI) (**www.scbwi.org**)

Further Reading

On writing and publishing

A Basic Guide to Writing, Selling, and Promoting Children's Books: Plus Information About Self-Publishing by Betsy B. Lee

Art and Fear: Observations on the Perils and Rewards of Artmaking by David Bayles and Ted Orland

The Artist's Way by Julia Cameron

The Art of Fiction: Notes on Craft for Young Writers by John Gardner

The Art of Writing for Children: Skills and Techniques of the Craft by Connie C. Epstein

An Author's Guide to Children's Book Promotion by Susan Salzman

Becoming a Writer by Dorothea Brande

The Craft of Writing a Novel by Phyllis Reynolds Naylor

Creating Characters Kids Will Love by Elaine Marie Alphin

The First Five Pages: A Writer's Guide to Staying Out of the Rejection Pile by Noah Lukeman

How to Get Your E-Book Published: An Insider's Guide to the World of Electronic Publishing by Richard Curtis and William Thomas Quick

How to Write and Sell Children's Picture Books by Jean E. Karl

Literary Market Place (LMP)

One Continuous Mistake by Gail Sher

On Writing: A Memoir of the Craft by Stephen King

Origins of Story: On Writing for Children, eds. Barbara Harrison and Gregory Maguire

Picture Writing: A New Approach to Writing for Kids and Teens by Anastasia Suen

Plotting and Writing Suspense Fiction by Patricia Highsmith

Poem-Making: Ways to Begin Writing Poetry by Myra Cohn Livingston

The Self-Publishing Manual by Dan Poynter

Steering the Craft, Exercises on Story Writing for the Lone Navigator or the Mutinous Crew by Ursula K. LeGuin

Take Joy: A Book for Writers by Jane Yolen

Writing a Novel by John Braine

Writing Books for Young People: New Expanded Edition by James Cross Giblin

Writing for Children & Teenagers by Lee Wyndham

Writing Down the Bones: Freeing the Writer Within by Natalie Goldberg

Writing for Young Children by Claudia Lewis

Writing Mysteries for Young People by Joan Lowery Nixon

Book lists and reviews

ALA Booklist

The Best Children's Books of the Year

BookPage

Bulletin of the Center for Children's Books

Caldecott Medal Books and Newbery Medal Books

Children's Choices and Young Adults' Choices
Children's Classics
The Horn Book Magazine
Kirkus Reviews
KLIATT Young Adult Paperback Book Guide
Notable Children's Books
Publishers Weekly
School Library Journal
VOYA, Voices of Youth Advocates

Marketing and other useful information
Children's Book Insider
Children's Writer
Children's Writer's and Illustrator's Market
Society of Children's Book Writers and Illustrators Bulletin

Useful Web sites
AgentQuery (**www.agentquery.com**)
Agent Research and Evaluation (**www.agentresearch.com**)
Association of Authors' Agents (Great Britain) (**www.agentsassoc.co.uk**)
Association of Authors' Representatives (**www.aaronline.org**)
The Authors Guild (**www.authorsguild.org**)
Book Crossroads (**www.ebookcrossroads.com/epublisher.html**)
Bowker Bar Code (**www.bowker.com**)
Bowker Link (**www.bowkerlink.com**)
Canadian Society of Children's Authors, Illustrators, and Performers
(**www.canscaip.org**)
Cataloging in Publication (**http://cip.loc.gov**)
Children's Book Council (**www.cbcbooks.org**)
Children's Literature Network (**www.childrensliteraturenetwork.org**)
The Children's Literature Web Guide (**www.acs.ucalgary.ca/~dkbrown**)
The Colossal Directory of Children's Publishers (**www.signaleader.com**)
The Cooperative Children's Book Center, the University of Wisconsin
(**www.education.wisc.edu/ccbc**)
Elance (**www.elance.com**)

Graphic Artists Guild (**www.graphicartistsguild.org**)

The Institute of Children's Literature (**www.institutechildrenslit.com**)

ISBN (**www.isbn.org**)

Library of Congress (**http://loc.gov**)

Lightning Source (**www.lightningsource.com/**)

Machine-Readable Coding Guidelines for the U.S. Book Industry (**www.bisg.org/isbn-13/barcoding.html**)

PEN (**www.pen.org**)

Preassigned Control Numbers (**http://pcn.loc.gov**)

Preditors and Editors (**www.anotherealm.com/prededitors/peba.htm**)

Publishers Marketplace (**www.publishersmarketplace.com**)

The Purple Crayon (**www.underdown.org**)

Society of Children's Book Writers and Illustrators (SCBWI) (**www.scbwi.org**)

U.S. Copyright Office (**www.copyright.gov**)

U.S. Patent and Trademark Office (**www.uspto.gov**)

Writer Beware (**www.sfwa.org/beware**)

Writer's Market (**www.writersmarket.com**)

WritersNet (**www.writers.net**)

Writers Write (**www.writerswrite.com**)

Directory listings

Book Dealers Dropship Directory — For drop-shippers

Books in Print

Book Trade in Canada

Canadian Books in Print

Canadian Publishers Directory

Children's Writer's and Illustrator's Market

Guide to Literary Agents

International Directory of Little Magazines and Small Presses — For self-publishers and small press listings

Literary Market Place

Small Press Record of Books in Print

Writers Market

Bibliography

The Business of Writing for Children by Aaron Shepard. Los Angeles: Shepard Publications, 2000.

The Complete Idiot's Guide to Publishing Children's Books by Harold D. Underdown. 3rd ed. New York: Alpha Books, 2008.

The Elements of Style by William Strunk, Jr. and E. B. White. 4th ed. New York: Macmillan Publishing Co., Inc., 2000.

The Encyclopedia of Writing and Illustrating Children's Books by Desdemona McCannon, Sue Thornton, and Yadzia Williams. Philadelphia: Running Press, 2008.

Friedman, Jane and Alice Pope, eds. *2009 Children's Writer's and Illustrator's Market.* 21st annual ed. Cincinnati, Ohio: F + W Books, 2008.

How to Publish Your Children's Book: A Complete Guide to Making the Right Publisher Say Yes by Liza N. Burby. Garden City Park, New York: Square One Publishers, 2004.

How to Write a Children's Book and Get It Published by Barbara Seuling. 3rd ed. Hoboken, New Jersey: John Wiley & Sons, Inc. 2005.

Jones, Alice, and Nick Clark. "The Independent Bath Literature Festival: Creative Writing Courses Are a Waste of Time, Says Hanif Kureishi." *The Independent.* Independent Digital News and Media, 3 Mar. 2014. Web. 10 May 2016.

Lamba, Marie. "10 Picture Book Pitfalls—and How to Fix Them." Editorial. *Writer's Digest* Mar.-Apr. 2016: 24-27. Print.

Self-Publishing Manual: How to Write, Print and Sell Your Own Book by Dan Poynter. 16th ed. Santa Barbara, California: Para Publishing, 2007.

Strategies for Teaching Boys and Girls--Secondary Level: A Workbook for Educators by Michael Gurian, Kathy Stevens, and Kelley King. San Francisco: Jossey-Bass, 2008.

Strawser, Jessica. "4 on 4." Editorial. *Writer's Digest* Mar.-Apr. 2016: 28-29. Print.

Unlocking Literacy: Effective Decoding & Spelling Instruction by Marcia K. Henry. Baltimore: Paul H. Brookes Publishing Co., 2003.

Weiland, K. M. "Most Common Writing Mistakes, Pt. 32: Boring Opening Lines." *Helping Writers Become Authors.* Helping Writers Become Authors, 03 Aug. 2014. Web. 10 May 2016.

Writing Children's Books for Dummies by Lisa Rojany Buccieri and Peter Economy. Hoboken, New Jersey: Wiley Publishing, 2005.

Glossary

Acquisitions editor: A member of a publishing company's staff that acquires manuscripts for publication.

Back matter: Material that appears in a book after the main text (i.e: bibliography, index, glossary, appendices, and the like); also called end matter.

Chapbook: Books first made in the 16th century by folding a single sheet of paper printed with text to make a book.

Characterization: The process by which the writer reveals the personality of a character.

CIP: A bibliographic record prepared by the Library of Congress for a book that has not yet been published; this record facilitates with book processing for libraries and book dealers.

Color theory: A body of practical guidance to color mixing and the visual impact of certain color combinations.

Cosplay: Combination of the words "costume" and "play," often used to refer to anime and manga fans that create their own costumes based on a certain character.

Cover letter: A letter sent with, and explaining the contents of, another document or package of materials or goods.

Division: A group of imprints that form a department of a publishing house.

Dummy book/Book dummy: A sample of a book; an informally bound book that is presented with representative illustrations.

E-publisher: A publisher that publishes digital copies of books, magazines, and the like.

Foreword: A brief introduction to a book, typically by a person other than the author of said book.

Galley: Proofs issued in the proofreading and copy-editing phase of book publishing.

Genre: A category of artistic composition, as in music or literature, characterized by similarities in form, style, or subject matter.

Graphic novel: Illustrated stories that differ from comics in that their stories tend to be of advanced complexity, like that of a novel; can be fiction or nonfiction.

Gutter: The inner margins of a bound book; the white space created by two facing pages in the center of the book near the binding.

Imprint: A specialized subdivision of a publishing house that focuses on a certain area and often carries a certain identity.

ISBN: International Standard Book Number; a unique, numeric commercial book identifier for booksellers.

LCCN: Library of Congress Control Number; these are used for authority, bibliographic, and classification records, and are currently structured according to length, elements, and position.

Leading: The space between printed lines.

Line: Part of an imprint at a publishing house that sometimes includes series of books.

Manga: Japanese comics, often for older youth and adult readers, but technically produced for young and old.

Megapublishers: Large, corporate conglomerate publishers, often based in New York City.

Mind-mapping: A diagram used to visually organize information.

Offset printing: A method of printing in which plates are used for ink printing.

Postpublication review: Intended for the consumer; appears after the book's release to the public.

Pre-writing: Anything you do to help the writing along, such as character outlines, brainstorming, and note taking.

Prepublication review: A review that releases before the book does.

Proposals: An argument for why your book is publishable; a business plan for your book.

Query letter: A single-page letter that introduces an author and his or her work.

Royalties: A sum of money paid to an author for each copy of a book sold.

Slush pile: A stack of unsolicited manuscripts that have been sent to a publishing company for consideration.

Spot color: Color generated by a single print run.

Storyboard: A sequence of boxes containing the words and images of a story—usually a picture book or graphic novel—that are similar to movie or television frames.

Submission package: A package sent to a publisher to showcase your work for publication consideration; usually contains a cover letter, a synopsis of your work, sample chapters from your manuscript, an author biography (particularly for nonfiction books), and a market analysis (also more common for nonfiction submissions).

Synopsis: A brief summary.

Trade publishers: Publishing companies that publish books typically found in bookstores.

Unsolicited/Unagented manuscript: Work that is without publisher solicitation or agent representation.

Index

About the Author

Rebekah Sack is a young adult nonfiction author. Her books cover topics such as bullying, interviewing, nutrition, confidence, and blogging. Her passion for helping teens survive the roller coaster of youth translates onto each page of her books. A summa cum laude graduate of Illinois State University, she now works for Atlantic Publishing Group as the in-house editor.